Seabiscuit

THE REST OF THE STORY

Best Wishes to Dick & Barb

Wm H Nichols

Seabiscuit
THE REST OF THE STORY

WILLIAM H. NICHOLS

TATE PUBLISHING & *Enterprises*

TATE PUBLISHING
& Enterprises

Tate Publishing is committed to excellence in the publishing industry. Our staff of highly trained professionals, including editors, graphic designers, and marketing personnel, work together to produce the very finest books available. The company reflects the philosophy established by the founders, based on Psalms 68:11,

"THE LORD GAVE THE WORD AND GREAT WAS THE COMPANY
OF THOSE WHO PUBLISHED IT."

If you would like further information, please contact us:

1.888.361.9473 | www.tatepublishing.com

TATE PUBLISHING & Enterprises, LLC | 127 E. Trade Center Terrace
Mustang, Oklahoma 73064 USA

This title is also available as a Tate Out Loud product.
Visit www.tatepublishing.com for more information

The opinions expressed by the author are not necessarily those of Tate Publishing, LLC.

This novel is a work of historical non-fiction. Several names, descriptions, entities and incidents included in the story are based on the lives of real people.

Published in the United States of America

ISBN: 978-1-6024729-8-3

07.03.12

For Lill, my wife, my partner and my best friend for fifty-eight years.

Acknowledgements

Shortly after the Seabiscuit movie was released in 2003, I was asked to give a talk to a charming chapter of "Red Hat" ladies at the home of Jo and Glenn Stabelfeld in Hughson, California. It was at that time that the seed, which germinated and grew into this book, was sown. I wish to express my thanks to that group.

Three years of research and interviews went into the project of writing the book *Seabiscuit–The Rest of the Story*. However, without the encouragement and assistance of numerous people, it would have been impossible to complete the task.

Foremost of those who helped me through the sometimes-discouraging attempts to gather data is my wife Lillian. Without her constant encouragement, I would most certainly have thrown in the towel many times. She and our daughter Kathy have been consistent in their confidence in the project.

Author Laura Hillenbrand has always been assuring in her belief that I had the ability to write the book. When I told her of my idea, her comment was, "Go for it." Her advice and suggestions have been priceless

Laverne Jones Booth, who spent her childhood on Ridgewood Ranch, provided me with a great deal of information about the Howard ranch as well as the human connections to the great Seabiscuit.

John Pollard, nephew of Red Pollard, provided insight into the character of his famous uncle and the entire Pollard family.

Thanks goes to my good friend Ray Land, who convinced me to contact Laura Hillenbrand when she was doing research for her best seller.

My friend and mentor, Walter Thomson, deserves special thanks for believing in us when we first contacted him about leasing his Thoroughbred breeding stock fifty years ago. He and his wife, Mary Jean, have been unwavering in their encouragement in this project.

Retired jockeys Clarence Tye and Tom Chapman graciously cooperated in the lengthy interviews for The "Bug Boys" chapter. They were able to give me an insight into the early trials and tribulations of an apprentice jockey on the "bush" circuits.

The encouragement and comments of Debbie Arrington, Sports writer for The Sacramento Bee, are greatly appreciated.

My interview with "Bud" Johnson provided me with information concerning the best sire among Seabiscuit's descendants, Windy Sea.

Tracy Livingston, President of the Board of Directors for The Seabiscuit Heritage Foundation has been a constant source of information and encouragement. It has been a delight knowing and working with him.

Jack Shinar, night/week-end editor for The Blood Horse magazine graciously agreed to write the foreword for the book.

Having such a prominent and talented writer endorse my efforts is greatly appreciated.

Ed. and Cindy Rose, residents of Ridgewood Ranch, are docents for and supporters of The Seabiscuit Heritage Foundation. Their extensive knowledge dealing with the history of the Howard ranch has been of great value to me.

The enthusiasm and encouragement expressed by Patrice West have meant more to me than she will ever know.

Special thanks goes to my special friends, Kay Conner, David Coffing, Doug Cross and LeAnn Lercari, who read my manuscript and made constructive criticisms that were incorporated into it.

And finally, my appreciation goes to my many good friends who have encouraged me to write this historical treatise about the great Seabiscuit and his human connections.

FOREWORD

*S*even decades after he thrilled racing fans from coast to coast, Seabiscuit remains the most famous horse in America. The people's champion captured the imagination of a new generation of racing fans, thanks to Laura Hillenbrand's best-selling biography and the 2003 Best Picture Oscar-nominated movie based on the lives of those who intersected with the amazing Thoroughbred's remarkable career.

Bill Nichols knows all about Seabiscuit. He didn't have to read about racing history; he lived it. As a teenager, Bill worked at Seabiscuit's home, Ridgewood Ranch, and learned to love the scrappy racehorse firsthand. . The Bay Area native had asked Seabiscuit's owner Charles Howard for a job where he could learn to work with horses. Mr. Howard gave him a dream apprenticeship at his ranch in Mendocino County.

Since then, Seabiscuit has been a central influence in Bill's life. On the first date with his future wife of 58 years, Bill took Lill to Seabiscuit's home. The couple became successful Thoroughbred breeders themselves at their Mares' Nest, the oldest racehorse nursery in Northern California. Their best horse was a grandson of Seabiscuit named Sea Orbit.

When Hillenbrand advertised for Seabiscuit experts while researching her book, Bill gave her a call. He became an important source and an inspiration for "Seabiscuit: An American Legend," the best selling sports book of all time.

That's how I met Bill and Lill, too. When searching for Seabiscuit experts for an article, he reached out to me. He was happy to share his saddle ride down memory lane and was generous with his time. His accounts were as vivid as if Seabiscuit ran last week, not scores of years ago.

As "Seabiscuit" the movie galloped along at the box office, Bill found his own phone ringing with requests. Long after his touch with stardom, he had become a local celebrity as the man who knew Seabiscuit. He repeatedly shared his stories with local school groups and equine fans, much to their delight. He helped spearhead the restoration of Ridgewood Ranch.

After much prodding, Bill decided to put his own recollections down on paper to share with future generations the rest of the Seabiscuit story. In these pages he recounts his tales of the famous horse's ranch days and the history behind the Howard's Willits hideaway. For fans that want to know more about this legendary 'Biscuit and his entourage, Bill completes the picture. In many ways, his *Seabiscuit, The Rest of the Story* comes straight from the horse's mouth.

In it, Bill explodes many of the myths surrounding the characters that were perpetuated in the process of making the movie. But just as often, I was struck by how his descriptions brought back vivid memories of scenes from the book and movie, images I suppose I will carry with me for the rest of my life.

But the whole gang is here–War Admiral and his owner Samuel Riddle and rider "The Dutchman" Charley Kurtsinger—as well as Seabiscuit's team of jockeys George Woolf and Red Pollard, trainer Tom Smith and, of course Charles and Marcela Howard. And there are so many more.

In addition, Bill offers a poignant chapter on author Laura Hillenbrand and her monumental battle with Chronic Fatigue Syndrome and vertigo, and the ongoing effort to restore the Howard ranch, given much impetus through publicity surrounding the book and film. Bill knows as much about the Thoroughbred breeding business as anyone I have encountered and he gives the reader the benefit of that knowledge in a straightforward discussion of Seabiscuit's bloodlines and all too brief stallion career.

Bill presents his fascinating tidbits in an easy-to-follow manner that makes for a quick and enjoyable read. I'm sure you'll agree that it answers many of the nagging questions about what happened to these folks after Seabiscuit's retirement from racing.

Jack Shinar
The Blood Horse

PREFACE

The March day was overcast and a light mist shrouded the giant redwood trees bordering highway 101 in Northern California. A custom made horse van made its way north on the beautiful two lane Redwood Highway, heading for Charles S. Howard's vast Ridgewood Ranch. The van was transporting precious cargo in the form of the great Seabiscuit. He had just become the world's leading money winning horse by annexing the Santa Anita Handicap on March 2nd, 1940.

Seabiscuit was returning to Ridgewood Ranch in order to resume his duties as a stallion. He had been bred to seven mares in the previous year, while recuperating from major injuries sustained in a Valentine's Day prep race for that year's Santa Anita Handicap. The resulting foals would become known as "The seven little Biscuits."

The story of Seabiscuit and his human connections returned the great racehorse to his previous fame through the best selling book *Seabiscuit: An American Legend* by author Laura Hillenbrand. The book was then made into a popular movie that received seven Academy Award nominations. However, the lives of Charles and Marcela Howard, Tom Smith, Red Pollard, George Woolf, War Admiral and the legendary champion did not end with the 1940 Santa Anita Handicap ... nor did Ridgewood Ranch, home of Seabiscuit.

These seven principals who contributed to the legend were from very diverse backgrounds. Their connections with one another were strictly chance meetings and the product of this relationship contributed to the success of Seabiscuit, each using his own unique talents. One additional person is the brilliant author, Laura Hillenbrand. She has been added to the previously mentioned group as without her research and literary talents, none of the group would be widely known today.

In her book, Laura devoted several chapters to biographical information regarding each of the characters. She deftly paints a background picture of each of the main characters with its flaws, its attributes, its humanity and the forces that drove it to success and sometimes to failure. Their lives became woven together with the common goal of proving to America that Seabiscuit was its greatest racehorse. Having succeeded in their quest, the tapestry of their lives began to unravel and each went separate ways. This book tells that story.

Contents

THE SEABISCUIT CONNECTION
ABOUT THE AUTHOR

*M*y connection with Seabiscuit, Ridgewood Ranch and Charles Howard began when, as a teenager, I wrote to Mr. Howard. I had decided at that young age that I eventually wanted to breed and raise Thoroughbred horses. I was born and raised in the San Francisco bay area and knew no one connected with the horse world, so it was an unlikely as well as an unexplainable goal, but a goal it was.

I realized that some practical experience and hands on training would be necessary and where better to obtain it than at Ridgewood Ranch, home of my equine idol, Seabiscuit?

I wrote to Mr. Howard, explaining my goal and addressed the letter to Ridgewood Ranch in Willits, California. Howard's residence and business was in San Francisco, so the letter was forwarded to him, back to the city in which it had originated.

Three days after mailing the letter, my phone rang. To my amazement, it was Mr. Howard apologizing for "taking so long to respond." Here was one of the wealthiest men west of the Mississippi River and he was personally calling a teen-age kid to apologize. He asked if I would come to his office at the Buick Agency on Van Ness Avenue so that he could meet me. I eagerly made an appointment.

My first impression of Mr. Howard was that "this man has class." It was an impression that never wavered during the time that I knew him.

When I arrived at the Buick Agency I was escorted to Mr. Howard's office. On the wall behind the desk was a large collage of the famous Seabiscuit/War Admiral match race, the focal point being the finish of the race.

We conversed at great length about my plans for the future and about his love for Seabiscuit and his beautiful Ridgewood Ranch. When interrupted by his secretary, he excused himself and briefly left the office, asking me to wait for his return. While he was away I spent the time looking at the various pictures and paintings adorning the walls of his office. I was especially intrigued by one large oil painting. It was of a young boy beside his dog. Obviously, I decided, it was a painting of a young Charles Howard.

When Howard returned I asked him if it was a painting of him as a boy. His eyes widened and he asked, "Do you think it looks like me?" I told him that I thought it did and his eyes welled with tears. "It is a painting of my son Frankie, who lost his life in an accident on Ridgewood Ranch," he said. I was horrified and embarrassed to have made this remarkable gentleman cry. Little did I know that more than fifty years later this embarrassing moment would give me a small amount of fame when Laura Hillenbrand included the incident in her famous book. That painting is currently prominently displayed in the Frank R. Howard Memorial Hospital in Willits, California. As for Howard, I decided, not only does he have class, but he is also a very sensitive and caring person.

I would discover, while working at Ridgewood, that he also had a sharp sense of humor. George Stemple, also a San Francisco businessman, had a neighboring ranch near Ridgewood. The four thousand acre expanse, named Willow Brook Ranch, was home to the Stemple stallion Put-In. While Put-In was admittedly a good Stakes winning racehorse, he was not in the same league as Seabiscuit. However, one Christmas, Stemple had a fictitious photo finish picture jerry-rigged, showing Put-In defeating Seabiscuit. He gave it to Howard as a Christmas gift. Howard enjoyed it so much that he had it framed and it hung in his Ridgewood dining room.

When we concluded the interview, which was really more of a visit between Seabiscuit admirers, he said that I was welcome to work at Ridgewood Ranch for as long as I wanted and that when I was ready to leave I could work at the racetrack with Tom Smith. I declined that opportunity, as the breeding, not the training part of the industry, was my principle interest. In retrospect, I now wish that I had taken the opportunity to work with Smith.

At Ridgewood I was given the responsibility of caring for seven mares and their foals as well as the stallion Vero. My favorite mares were Illeana and Gold Rim. Illeanna's daughter, Sea Flora, was to play an important part in my life a dozen years later.

After completing my Ridgewood education, I returned to the San Francisco Bay area and shortly thereafter I met and fell in love with the girl with whom I wanted to spend my life. She was also interested in horses, but the problem was that I couldn't convince her to go out with me. I tried everything I could think of. The movies, dining, dancing, they all elicited the same response, a polite "Thank you, but I don't think so." Finally

I got smart. "How would you like to drive up to Ridgewood Ranch to see the home of Seabiscuit," I said. She responded, "That sounds like fun." So again, Seabiscuit had a profound influence on my life. That was our first date and Lill and I will celebrate our fifty-ninth wedding anniversary in 2007. Thank you, again, Seabiscuit.

My next connection was as co-breeder of the fine Stakes horse Sea Orbit with my good friend Walter Thomson. More about that in the "Baby Biscuit" chapter. There was minimal Seabiscuit influence until my chance contact with Laura Hillenbrand, as described in the chapter titled "The Restoration." During the intervening years my wife and I had both obtained our college degrees and were working toward establishing our family with son Bob and daughter Kathy, as well as building our Thoroughbred breeding farm, which we named Mares' Nest.

Now retired, I serve on the Board of Directors for both the California Thoroughbred Breeders Association and the Seabiscuit Heritage Foundation and we continue to operate Mares' Nest.

The painting of Frankie Howard was originally in his father's office, but now hangs in The Frank R. Howard Memorial Hospital in Willits, California.
Photo by the author.

THE "ADMIRAL" ARRIVES

At the time, May 2, 1934 appeared to be just another spring day at Faraway Farm in Lexington, Kentucky. The majority of the 1934 foal crops were already stretching their legs in mock races around the lush bluegrass pastures.

There were a few late foals yet to be born and on May 2, one of these was a small, plain brown colt. With little to distinguish him from his bigger, flashier relatives, his arrival was significant only to his dam, Brushup. This was the second foal of the royally bred daughter of the great stallion Sweep. For the most part, the offspring of Sweep tended to be on the small side. Brushup was no exception. At 14 hands 3 ¾ inches, describing her as "small" was a gross understatement. The accepted measurement of a horse is designated as a "hand." A hand is four inches and the measurement is taken from the withers to the ground. Brushup, at 59 ¾ inches was slightly less than five feet in height. The Thoroughbred establishment would consider this measurement on the small side.

Her trim little foal was the result of a mating with the

magnificent Man O' War. Man O' War was larger than life in every aspect. The fiery chestnut so dominated the horses with which he raced, that he was retired as a three year old. His size, his temperament and his immense stride had simply run him out of competition. Dubbed "Big Red" by his fans, he was described as "de mostest hoss dat ever was" by his faithful groom Will Halbut. In the 1970's, as a compliment to the great Man O' War, another chestnut phenomenon, Secretariat, would also be called "Big Red."

Man O' War retired with twenty wins from twenty-one starts. His lone loss, after being compromised by a poor start, was to a horse that ironically was named Upset. At the time that Man O' War was racing there were no starting gates. The horses would walk up to the starting line, circle, and line up and await the starter's flag. Man O' War was still circling when the flag fell. He was, in fact, facing the wrong direction. By the time he aligned himself, the field of horses had attained a tremendous advantage and the great "Big Red" set off after them with a near impossible task before him. It is especially difficult to make up ground in a sprint race of six furlongs. A furlong is one eighth of a mile, making this race, The Sanford Stakes, only 3/4ths of a mile in length. To further complicate the task, jockey Loftus tried to save ground by racing close to the rail. This is the logical tactic, but, in this case, it proved to be a fatal one. Man O' War amazingly caught up with the field, but became boxed in and had to be checked. He had to go around horses to the outside and attempt another run at the leaders. It was too much to ask of the great champion. He ran out of ground and suffered the only loss of his career by a quickly diminishing one half-length.

At three, Man O' War proved unbeatable, winning all eleven of his starts and giving away large amounts of weight to his competitors. Despite carrying top weight his winning margins were incredible. He won races by twenty lengths and by as much as one hundred lengths. Riddle decided to retire his champion when he was informed that he would have to carry weights of 145 to 150 pounds during his four-year-old career.

Riddle, born in Pennsylvania, owned a 17,000-acre farm in Maryland; it was Named GlenRiddle Farm. He used the one-mile track for training purposes. The farm was also used for Riddles passion for fox hunting. Man O' War had started his training career here and was rested at GlenRiddle between his two and three year old campaigns. It was to this farm that he was sent in order to let down after his racing career was completed. The following January he was moved to Faraway Farm in Kentucky.

Man O' War proved to be an outstanding sire, despite the fact that his owner, Samuel Riddle, limited his chances by allowing only a few outside mares to be bred to him each year. For the most part he was bred only to Riddle's own mares. Big Red lived a long life, dying on November 1, 1947 at the age of thirty. His grandson Seabiscuit had died in May of the same year and his famed lifelong groom, Will Harbut, preceded Man O'War in death by only a month. "Big Red" was buried in his paddock on Faraway Farm, but his remains were eventually moved to The Kentucky Horse Park in Lexington, Kentucky.

The mating of Brushup to Man O' War had a strange beginning. It is reported that Luther Burbank, the famous botanist and geneticist, had observed that many great human offspring were the product of older men and younger women. He wondered if this could also be effective when breeding horses. The word was passed on to Scott, the manager of Faraway Farm. He convinced Riddle to allow him to make the Man O'War–Brushup cross, despite the fact that Riddle did not favor the mare.

Riddle was a very opinionated man with his own ideas concerning breeding theories. He had a very different attitude and temperament than did Charles Howard. While Riddle had a tendency to be arrogant and self-centered, Howard was a sensitive man with a great deal of compassion for his fellow man.

The Man O' War–Brushup colt was so different, in every way, from his famous sire, that few would have the temerity to suggest that he would become Man O'War's greatest son. Nevertheless, he was given a name that befitted his royal breeding and predicted his brilliant future. War Admiral had arrived.

Sometime, between his entry into the world and his yearling year, War Admiral had developed from an insignificant looking foal into an impressive colt. He was eagerly waiting for the time when he would be able to prove to the racing world that he was, indeed, a well-named future champion.

He was never the powerhouse, in conformation, that his sire was. Instead, he was a lithe, well-balanced individual. His stride was smooth and he flowed over the fields with an effortless action. One genetic trait, inherited from his male line, was the fiery temper of Man O' War. He, in turn, had kept that flame alive from his father, Fair Play and Fair Play's sire, the willful Hastings. If there was anything that this brilliant male line lacked, it was patience. Their fiery competitive nature manifested itself with their eagerness to get on with the race. Forget this nonsense of walking quietly around the saddling paddock and who came up with the ridiculous act of parading up and down, in front of the grandstand, in postposition order? The Man O' War tribe should always be leading the pack. And what about the starting gate? That was the most idiotic idea yet. War Admiral was such a notoriously bad actor that he was the bane of starters wherever he raced.

By the time that he reached his two-year-old season, War

Admiral had become civilized enough to begin his racing career. And what a brilliant career it was to become. On April 25, 1936 he made his first start. His trainer, George Conway, entered him in a 4-½ furlong maiden event against nine other juveniles. He ran a close second for most of the race, finishing strongly taking the lead by the slim margin of a nose at the wire. The lack of confidence felt by the betting public was evidenced by the payoff of $17.00 for a $2.00 bet.

On May 21, at Belmont Park, he was entered against winners in a five-furlong allowance race. His maiden win did not appear to impress the bettors as he was allowed to get off at odds of 10 to 1. He led the other seven colts wire to wire, winning by three lengths in a style that would become his trademark. His winning time was a brilliant 58–4/5 for the five furlongs.

This was enough to convince the public. When War Admiral came out for his first Stakes attempt, on June 6 in Belmont Park's National Stallion Stakes, he was bet down to 3 to 1 for the five furlong event. For some reason, whether it was instructions from the trainer or the idea of his jockey, he was taken back at the start and asked to close ground in the stretch. Oops! It didn't work. He closed ground, but could not catch the brilliant Pompoon, running third to that two-year-old champion by 2-½ lengths. That was to be the last time that the great jockey, Jack Westrope, was to ride War Admiral. Charlie Kurtsinger became his regular rider when he made his next start in the 6 furlong Great American Stakes on July 1. He took the lead immediately, but tired and finished second. Given a little more time between races, he won the Eastern Shore Handicap by five lengths. The chart described it as "easily." On October 10, he finished out his two-year-old season with a second in a Stake at Laurel Race Course in Maryland.

He went off as the favorite for the first time in his career. He would never again race as anything but the favorite.

In six starts as a two year old, War Admiral compiled the excellent record of 3 wins, 2 seconds and a third. He was assigned 121 pounds on the Experimental Free Handicap, ranking him the fifth best two year old in The United States. Pompoon was assigned top weight and the Championship.

There were three high quality two year olds, sired by Man O' War, in 1936. According to American Race Horses–1936, John Hervey, the famous author who used the pen name of "Salvator," called the three brilliant juveniles "The Man O' War Flotilla." They were Matey, the filly Wand and War Admiral. Following War Admiral's October 10 race, he was given six months to relax and mature.

It was spring, the year was 1937 and what a drama filled year it was to become … It began with the great Louisville (Home of The Kentucky Derby) flood that left thousands homeless. John D. Rockefeller, the great philanthropist who gave away over 700 million dollars in his lifetime, died. The dirigible Hindenberg exploded. Joe Louis became the heavyweight champion. Amelia Earhart disappeared over the Pacific and War Admiral was to become a Triple Crown winner. On April 14 he made his first start as a three year old, winning "in hand" by 2 ½ lengths. He was on his way and had dead aim on the coveted Triple Crown races. Starting one more time prior to the Kentucky Derby, he won The Chesapeake by six lengths. His win was described as "easily best."

Two weeks later he would go forth as the favorite in The Kentucky Derby, beating his two-year-old nemesis, Pompoon, by 1-¾ lengths. A week later he came back in the Preakness Stakes, on a "good" track, and again bested Pompoon. This time he won by only a head.

After a three-week break, the scene shifted to Belmont

Park. War Admiral captured The Triple Crown by winning The Belmont Stakes by three lengths in track record time. Daily Racing Form said that War Admiral was "easily best."

As easy as the winning of The Belmont Stakes appeared, it was a traumatic event for War Admiral. In this, the third leg of the coveted Triple Crown, War Admiral's horrible gate manners delayed the start by nearly nine minutes. When the starter's bell rang he literally leaped out of the gate. In so doing the toe of his hind shoe hit the heel of his right fore hoof. A square inch of his heel was left on the track and a trail of blood followed his run to victory.

Unlike many of our recent three-year-old champions, War Admiral was not retired to rest on his ample laurels. Given a much-deserved rest, he returned on October 26 to win three more races in only an eight-day period.

As a three-year-old, War Admiral had developed into a sleek, elegant running machine. He was measured at precisely 15 hands 2 ¼ inches at the time of the classics.

His undefeated three-year-old season assured War Admiral of being acclaimed "Horse of the Year in 1937."

War Admiral's four-year-old racing career began on February 19 at Florida's Hialeah Park. He won and came back in March to win The Widener Handicap by 1 ½ lengths, "eased up," after leading by five lengths. June saw him winning a Stakes race at New York's Aqueduct, carrying an impressive 132 pounds.

Three weeks later he traveled to Suffolk Downs for The Massachusetts Handicap. He carried 130 pounds on a "heavy" track and met his first defeat in over twenty months, terminating an eleven race-winning streak.

July saw him back on another muddy track at Saratoga. He won this one as "much best" by eight lengths. Three days later, packing 130 pounds, he defeated the great mare Esposa by a neck on a sloppy track. After two more wins over Esposa, he won The Saratoga Cup "easily" by four lengths.

Next on War Admiral's menu was The Pimlico Special on November 1. This race would go down in history as The Race of the Century. The four-length win, by Seabiscuit, became the most famous race in history, its flame rekindled by Laura Hillenbrand's classic book. *The Daily Racing Form* commented, regarding War Admiral's loss, "No excuse."

Eleven days later, War Admiral won The Rhode Island Handicap, eased up by 2 ½ lengths. This was his last race in 1938. Seabiscuit was acclaimed as the 1938 Champion.

The Admiral was to start one more time. With a change of jockeys, he won an allowance race on February 18 at Hialeah and was then retired.

War Admiral was one of America's greatest racehorses. He was just not quite as great a racehorse as Seabiscuit, but then few have achieved that level. This should not diminish his considerable achievements. He proved to be a very accomplished sire, leading the sire list in 1945. That was the year that his great daughter Busher was voted Horse of the Year. His sons War Jeep and Mr. Busher were also major Stakes Winners. Additionally, he was also a great broodmare sire, leading that list in 1962 and 1964. War Admiral's daughters and their offspring read like a Who's Who for the Thoroughbred breed. They include several who are considered among the greatest. Busher, Searching, Crafty Admiral, Iron Maiden (dam of Kentucky Derby winner Iron Liege and grandam of Kentucky Derby winner Swaps) and Busanda, dam of the incomparable Buckpasser are all sired by War Admiral or out of War Admiral mares. Although he didn't defeat Seabiscuit on the racetrack, he far outdid him in the breeding shed.

War Admiral died in 1959 and is buried beside his sire at The Kentucky Horse Park.

War Admiral

Brown Horse – 1934

Sire: Man O' War by Fair Play
Dam: Brushup by Sweep
Breeder: Samuel D. Riddle (Kentucky)
Owner: Glen Riddle Farm Stable
Trainer: G. Conway

Lifetime Race Record

At two – 1936: 6 starts – 3 wins – 2 seconds – 1 third
At three – 1937: 8 starts – 8 wins
At four – 1938: 11 starts – 9 wins – 1 second – 1 fourth
At five – 1939: 1 start – 1 win

Lifetime: 26 starts – 21 wins – 3 seconds – 1 third – 1 fourth
Total earnings $273,240

Winner of The Triple Crown
 (Kentucky Derby, Preakness Stakes & Belmont Stakes)

War Admiral, Charles Kurtsinger up.
Photo courtesy of *The California Thoroughbred* magazine

THE RESTORATION

According to Webster, to "restore" is "to reproduce as originally existing, as in a work of art or an extinct animal." This is what author Laura Hillenbrand accomplished with her book "Seabiscuit: An American Legend." The passing of the years had dimmed the public's memory of the great Thoroughbred, along with that of his human connections. Hillenbrand's book reminded older Americans of the depression era and the effect that under-dog Seabiscuit's rise from obscurity to world acclaim had on the American public. For those who are too young to have experienced the phenomenon it became a learning experience, an awakening and a revelation. For all of us, Seabiscuit, The Howards, Smith, Pollard, Woolf and War Admiral were restored to their former brilliance. Without Laura, none of these entities would today be well known, excepting by a handful of people who lived the story with them.

Spring is a time of excitement and anticipation in the Thoroughbred world. Newly arrived foals carry the hopes and dreams of their human connections. In Kentucky, within the month of May, both Seabiscuit and War Admiral had first seen the light of day. Three decades later, in northern Virginia, in the early evening of May 15, 1967 Bernard and Elizabeth Hillenbrand became the proud parents of a newborn "filly." They named her Laura.

Laura grew up in Bethesda, Maryland, about eight miles from her present home in Washington D.C. She, and her brother John, and sisters Lisa and Susan, enjoyed life on the family farm and Laura spent countless hours riding bareback in the cow pastures. As with many young girls, horses became an important part of her life and as a teenager she was an accomplished rider. She showed the Thoroughbred gelding, Double Fault, over jumps in the local horse shows. Double Fault, a winning racehorse, was born the same year as Laura. It would make a great story if I could say that he was a descendant of Seabiscuit or Man O' War or even of War Admiral. Alas, it was not to be. The only connection he could lay claim to is through Whisk Broom 11. Seabiscuit was out of a daughter of that famous stallion and Double Fault was line-bred with three crosses to Whisk Broom 11.

Laura's teen years were typical of a bright, energetic young horsewoman. She rode and showed her filly Allspice, who had been rescued from slaughter by Laura and her sister Susan. Laura was an excellent student and a good athlete, swimming competitively in the 100-meter backstroke and she was also an avid tennis player. She had always been interested in writing and, as she said: "I was born a writer." Not a surprise. She was genetically programmed for the career. Her father was the Executive Director of a Washington lobbying group, a position, like writing, which demands a great deal of research work. Her mother was a psychologist and former journalist for the Washington Post.

Despite the obvious affinity for becoming a historical

researcher and writer, she chose to major in English and history, with the goal of becoming a history professor. Her choice of colleges was Kenyon College in Gambier, Ohio. Gambier is about four hundred miles from her home in Bethesda, Maryland and fifty plus miles northeast of Columbus, Ohio. She was a sophomore, a straight-A student, had a caring, handsome boy friend and life was good. That is, until the unthinkable occurred.

On March 20, 1987, the nineteen-year-old college student was driving back to campus, from Washington D.C., with her boy friend Borden Flanagan. The couple stopped at a fast food restaurant and Laura became violently ill after eating some bad chicken. By the time they reached the college, she was in such bad shape that her friends called the paramedics. The effects of the food poisoning continued for days. Her attempt to return to classes failed. Her energy level was at zero and within two weeks she could not even sit up in bed. She found it difficult to speak and returned home to live with her mother. It would be an agonizingly long stretch of time before her ailment was correctly diagnosed.

She was examined by doctor after doctor. She would have high fevers several times a day. She had swollen lymph nodes and lost twenty-three pounds. Not knowing what caused her illness, they tested her for multiple sclerosis and AIDS. Both proved negative. Doctors came up with numerous incorrect answers to her problem. Some of which were that it was psychosomatic, she was bulimic or perhaps it was simply a symptom of adolescence. Laura said, "I definitely had a lot of problems with people thinking that this is some sort of hypochondria or some sort of willful attempt to get attention." She was also accused of using it to get out of attending classes, despite the fact that she was a straight-A student.

Finally, a correct diagnosis was obtained. The Johns Hopkins University, in Baltimore, Maryland was founded in 1876 and was the first research University in the United States. Laura discovered that what she had was Chronic Fatigue Syndrome, referred to as CFS for short. The diagnostician was Dr. John Bartlett, who was Chief of Staff of Infectious Diseases. The disease affects about 800,000 of the population in the United States, but in varying degrees of severity. Even with a correct diagnosis, many people mistakenly think it is just a case of severe laziness.

In 1987, upon his graduation from college, Borden moved in with Laura and her mother. Eventually, Laura and her fiancé Borden moved to Chicago where he pursued his graduate degree, but Laura's health again deteriorated. During a visit with her mother she became so ill that she was unable to return to Chicago and remained in Maryland. Borden returned to Chicago, completed his education and returned to be with Laura. Gradually Laura improved and by 1990 she felt up to flying to Seattle to meet Borden's parents. The following year, Laura, accompanied by Borden and some friends, decided to travel to Saratoga Racetrack in New York. It was a disastrous decision. On their return, she was hit with severe chills and fever and went into shock. Her reaction was so severe that she spent months when she was unable to do such simple tasks as rolling over in bed. For two months she was unable to go down stairs. She suffered severe vertigo, which plagued her all through the writing of her book and continues to be a major problem for her.

In 1995, her fiancé Flanagan, having graduated from college, moved to Washington D. C. to be with Laura. They have been together ever since that time. He is currently a professor of political theory at American University. Laura recently stated, in an article by Washington Post correspondent Jennifer Frey, "I am the most blessed person on earth. I really am, because I have him. He is compassionate, understanding. He shrugs off all my flaws- and I have a mountain of them-and loves me anyway. I'm still madly in love with him."

Laura has long been a Seabiscuit admirer. As a child she bought a young adults book titled "Come on Seabiscuit." Who would have predicted that her seventy-five cent purchase would change and direct her future? She read and re-read it and she still has the well-worn copy. In 1996 she was researching some old racing documents and re-discovered Seabiscuit. She found the information about the horse, Howard, Smith and Pollard so interesting that she was certain that there was a book waiting to be written.

She spent four years researching the story. She consulted record books, films, photographs, newspapers, magazines, and advertised in equine magazines to interview anyone who had a personnel connection with any of the major characters during the saga of the great Seabiscuit. That's where I came into the story. My good friend, Ray Land, had clipped an ad from *The Thoroughbred Times*, requesting that anyone who had experienced any personal contact with Seabiscuit, Howard, Smith, Pollard or Woolf, contact her by e-mail. I must admit that I ignored the request for several weeks. Finally, I got tired of Ray's asking me if I had responded. So, I did so just to keep him quiet. What a good decision and what a good friend to keep after me until I made that decision.

Laura once said, "I think the secret to bringing immediacy to any nonfiction story is to ferret out every detail that is there to be found, so that the reader feels like an eyewitness." This she did. It wasn't easy. Interviews were conducted when Laura was relatively free from the constant vertigo and exhaustion. If she could sit up in bed, she would interview or research or write. If not, she would, at times, lie in bed with her laptop.

She arranged for libraries to send her books and newspapers needed for her research.

In a 2003 *New York Times* article, Laura stated, "My other major obstacle was vertigo, which causes my surroundings to look and feel like they are spinning or pitching up and down. The symptoms never go away, but reading and writing greatly exacerbates them, as does looking down. My boyfriend jerry-rigged a device to hold source materials upright, so I could avoid looking down. I put my laptop on a stack of books, so it was at eye level. When the vertigo was very bad, I'd lie in bed and write on a pad with my eyes closed. It was punishing work. At the end of the day I was quite nauseated from the vertigo and exhaustion, and in the final weeks of writing I was so overworked that my hands shook, but I got the book done. I did not take good care of myself as I wrote this book, and I'm continuing to pay for it. The day after I turned in my manuscript, my health collapsed. My exhaustion became much more severe, and my vertigo returned in force, making it impossible to read more than a few lines a day."

Random House published "Seabiscuit: an American Legend" in March of 2001. I treasure my copy of the book, given to me by Laura and inscribed, "To Bill Nichols, with immense gratitude for all your help and friendship as I wrote this book. Much love, Laura." It was an immediate success. It shot to the top of the New York Times Best Seller List and remained there for thirty-six weeks. That was just the hard cover issue. The paperback remained on the list for 120 weeks. More than two and a half million copies were printed.

The precursor to the Seabiscuit book was her 1988 *American Heritage* article on Seabiscuit. It won the Eclipse Award for Magazine Writing, the highest journalistic honor in Thoroughbred racing. Due to the article, Random House contracted to publish the book, as yet unwritten, and Hillenbrand was able to sell foreign publishing rights, as well as the movie rights to Universal Studios. The book has been sold in fifteen languages. In 2001 she was winner of the Turf Publicists of America's Big Sport of Turfdom award. Past recipients of the award include Bill Shoemaker, Burt Bacharach, Steve Cauthen, Jack Klugman, John Forsythe, Tim Conway, Jim McKay and Laffit Pincay Jr. Laura was in elite company and she was a well deserved addition. Also, in 2001, she received her second Eclipse award. This was one for Feature/Enterprise Writing. Additionally, the book was the winner of the Booksense Nonfiction Book of the Year Award and the William Hill Sports Book of the year in Great Britain. It was also a finalist for the National Book Critics Circle Award, the Los Angeles Book Prize, the Barnes and Noble Discover Award and the Borders Original Voices Award. Sadly, Laura's health kept her from attending any of the award ceremonies.

Laura treasures a personal letter she received in June of 2001, from former President George Bush! He said that George W. had urged him to read the book, and that he complied and "absolutely loved it." He continued, "I expect everyone says I couldn't put it down, but in my case, that is true." He asked her to sign his copy for their private library. Four Presidents have read the Hillenbrand book as well as countless others throughout the world, but not only is she a talented writer, but also she is modest and unassuming about her accomplishments.

The movie rights for her book were sold before the book was published; such was the publicity and interest after she won an Eclipse Award for her magazine article dealing with Seabiscuit. Laura was very selective in her choice of Universal Studios and Gary Ross to turn her book into a motion picture. She wanted to be certain that the story would be told as she had written it. The movie, discussed in another chapter, was a huge success.

Because of her health problem, Laura was unable to travel and attend a premiere of the Seabiscuit movie. The three premieres were located in Saratoga, New York, Hollywood, California and Willits, California. Living in Washington, D.C., the long trips were out of the question. George and Laura Bush to the rescue. The President and First Lady invited Laura, Borden and the stars and producer of the movie to dine at The White House and attend a special premiere. "It was the greatest night of my life," said Laura. Bush, his eyes swelling with tears, thanked Laura for "writing a fantastic book about America." "I felt so moved I couldn't say a thing," the author recalled.

In 2004 Laura became involved with Operation Iraqi Children. In December of 2003, the day of Suddam Hussein's capture, Army Lt. Col. Sherman McGrew wrote a note to Laura, from Iraq. He and his fellow soldiers had been attempting to bring assistance to Iraqi schools. The schools lacked even the most basic supplies of books and blackboards. He had taken a "single dog-eared" copy of her book to a girl's school and noticed that the students were fascinated by the story. He had read it to them during a mortar attack. The girls wanted to know more about the man that had written this wonderful book. When they were told that "Laura" was a woman, they couldn't believe that a female would be allowed to write a book. Unfortunately, at that time there were no copies in the Iraqi language. Hillenbrand and McGrew, through her Arabic language publisher in Egypt, arranged to have copies sent to the children. Word spread and donations began coming in. "The response was extraordinary," said Hillenbrand. Actor Gary Sinise, after touring Iraqi, had founded an effort to bring school supplies to Iraqi children. Soon, he and Laura discovered that they shared a common goal and combined their programs. The program is still co-run by Hillenbrand and Sinise and is now entirely devoted to providing school supplies.

Laura sacrificed her health in order to write her book, but she feels that it was not too high a price to pay as it has allowed her to become an advocate for, and make the public aware of, the greatly misunderstood and serious disease, Chronic Fatigue Syndrome.

THE 3 RIDERS

CHARLES E. KURTSINGER, nicknamed "The Dutch-man," rode War Admiral in nineteen of the champi-on's twenty-six races. They included nearly all of the most important wins, including the Triple Crown races and the famous Seabiscuit/War Admiral match race.

The Dutchman was born on November 16, 1906 in Shep-herdsville, Kentucky. He came close to winning another Triple Crown when he rode Twenty Grand to wins in the Kentucky Derby and Belmont Stakes, but finished second in the Preak-ness. He also rode Head Play to his 1933 Preakness win as well as wins in the Bay Meadows, San Antonio and San Juan Capistrano Handicaps in California. He was not on Head Play in the Kentucky Derby when what turned out to be one of the most famous racing pictures in history was taken. The two horses came down the stretch, head for head, in a tight struggle. But, the struggle between the horses was nothing compared to the one between the two jockeys. As they came around the far turn, heading into the stretch, Head Play bore out and brushed with Broker's Tip. Meade, Broker's Tips' jockey and Fisher, on

Head Play, began lashing out at one another. The battle went on for the length of the stretch with Broker's Tip winning by the shortest of noses. This resulted in the only win of Broker's Tip's career. If you're only going to win one race in your career, it's not a bad time to do it. The photographer clicked his camera just as they were crossing the finish line and the historical picture was captured. The Stewards made no change in the finish of the race, but both jockeys were suspended and The Dutchman inherited the ride on Head Play in future races.

Kurtsinger rode War Admiral only once after the November 1st, 1938 match race with Seabiscuit. That was on November 12 when he won the Rhode Island Handicap by 2 ½ lengths, carrying 127 pounds. At that time Riddle publicly announced that he was taking Kurtsinger off of War Admiral and replacing him with jockey W. D. Wright. Kurtsinger, unwisely, had publicly stated that he blamed the match race defeat on "too much cup-racing" for War Admiral. "Cup" races are long distance races and they have all but disappeared on the American racing scene. War Admiral had run in races of 2 miles and 1-¾ miles shortly prior to the match race. The Dutchman felt that these races had dulled War Admiral's natural speed. Conway, War Admiral's trainer, took this as a criticism for his failing to give the horse a short prep race, or at least some fast workouts prior to the match. Conway and Riddle did not take the criticism lightly. Shortly thereafter, Kurtsinger retired from riding after experiencing a fall. He rode briefly the following year, 1939, and then retired permanently from his riding career to become a trainer.

In his fifteen year riding career he rode 721 winners from 5,651 mounts. He won two of each of the Triple Crown races and was the leading money-winning jockey in 1931 and 1937. Kurtsinger was elected to the National Museums Hall of Fame in 1967. He died, at the age of thirty-nine on September 24,

1946. The cause of death was listed as complications due to pneumonia.

GEORGE M. WOOLF: Flamboyant, gregarious, generous, dedicated and a perfectionist. These are just a few of the words that come to mind when describing the great jockey. He was all of these and more.

Born in 1910, he was genetically programmed to become a rider. His Mother performed circus acrobatics on horses and his Father was a stagecoach driver. At the age of eighteen, George began his riding career in Montana. It was during his early years of riding on the "bush" tracks, the minor leagues of racing, when he met, and became a lifelong friend of future Seabiscuit rider, Red Pollard.

Woolf was a perfectionist when it came to race riding. He would spend extensive amounts of time researching the races in which he had mounts. He memorized the details of his competitors. That included the other riders as well as the horses against which he was to compete and he used that knowledge to visualize how the race would likely be run. He was thus able to plan the ride on his horse and determine when to make a winning move. His nickname "The Iceman" was attained by his uncanny ability to keep a cool head during a race and not panic. He developed the ability to time his horse's move, waiting until the maximum moment of opportunity, so that he could reach the finish line at precisely the correct time. In racing parlance, he had a "clock in his head." He became noted for the fact that many of his finishes resulted in a photo finish. Due to this ability he set an amazing record of not losing a photo finish, in a Stakes race, for a period of ten years.

"The Iceman" enjoyed life to the fullest. His flamboyance was legendary. Sporting tailor made western suits and shirts, handcrafted silver mounted western boots and topped by his ever-present ten-gallon hat, he was a sight long remembered. Cruising around in his custom made Studebaker road-ster, George was the envy of other jockeys and the handsome rider attracted lovely young females like flies to honey. At age twenty- one, he married a beautiful sixteen-year-old waitress named Genevieve. They remained married until his death.

In sharp contrast to Woolf's carefree attitude, he harbored a dark secret. He kept secret the fact that he had suffered from diabetes for many years. His struggle to maintain the weight necessary for him to perform as a rider required him to adhere to a diet that was in stark contrast to that which was recommended by his doctor. This was in the early, experimental years of insulin therapy and the scientific knowledge was not such that the dosages were always prescribed correctly. Despite the fact that he gave himself daily insulin injections, he had reactions that he attempted to hide from those who were close to him. He would often, and suddenly, fall asleep. Friends attributed it to just another of George's idiosyncrasies and he did nothing to dispel their assumption.

Due to his health problems and his dieting, he eventually limited his rides to an average of four or five a week. His popularity and talent were so enormous that he was able to select his mounts and ride some of the finest horses available. A few of the great horses Wolff rode, in addition to Seabiscuit, were Whirlaway, Challedon, Alsab, Gallorette, Kayak II, Bold Venture and Pompoon. He considered Seabiscuit to be the best horse he ever rode.

The list of important Stakes won by Woolf is impressive. He won three consecutive Hollywood Gold Cups, three consecutive American Derbies, The Preakness, The Brooklyn Handicap and numerous other great races. He won a total of 721 races from only 3,784 rides for an impressive 19.1% win record.

The Iceman's famed generosity became his undoing. At

California's Santa Anita Park in 1946, a friend asked him to ride for him. Although he was feeling ill, he obliged. His generosity was legendary and he rarely refused a friend a favor. His illness, that day, was undoubtedly a result of his diabetes, combined with his destructive diet. As the field of horses rounded the first turn, George Woolf appeared to lose consciousness, slipped from the saddle and crashed head first to the ground directly in the path of the other runners. He never regained consciousness and was dead at the young age of thirty-five. Nearly two thousand mourners, many of them Hollywood celebrities, attended his funeral. When film star Gene Autry sang "Empty Saddles in the Old Corral" there wasn't a dry eye in the crowd.

In his honor the George Woolf Memorial Jockey Award has been given annually since 1985. The award goes to riders whose careers and personal character reflect positively on themselves and the sport of Thoroughbred racing. It is prized as one of racings most prestigious accolades.

A statue of George (The Iceman) Woolf stands, along with the famed statue of Seabiscuit, in the gardens of Santa Anita Park.

FARRELL (WILD HORSE) JONES:

Born in Idaho in 1922, Farrell Jones never had the opportunity to ride Seabiscuit in a race, but he is certainly one of the last remaining personal links with the champion.

Jones began riding racehorses at the tender age of nine and in 1935, as a teen-ager, he left his native state and headed for Southern California. His reputation was such that the Howard Stable signed him as an apprentice rider. This was shortly prior to the time that Howard purchased Seabiscuit. In fact, Jones was present in August of 1936 when Seabiscuit arrived at the Howard barn. It was at that time that he made his now famous comment "Looks like they got another saddle horse."

Seabiscuit's jockey, Red Pollard, gave the "Wild Horse" moniker to Jones and the youngster became a regular rider of The Biscuit in the morning gallops and workouts. He continued riding him until Seabiscuit's retirement in 1940. This long relationship, with the horse, gives credence to his comments regarding Seabiscuit's temperament. In the forward of Barbara Howard's book "Letters to Seabiscuit," he said that "Anybody could gallop Seabiscuit, anyone could breeze him. He was a big gentle kitten, and he did everything just the way it was supposed to be done. A very, very intelligent horse."

With the retirement of the Champion and the advent of World War II, Jones joined the Navy as a deep-sea diver. When his time in the service was finished, the former eighty-pound youngster had become too heavy to continue his riding career. His decision to become a trainer of Thoroughbreds was a wise one. His lifelong work with racehorses, coupled with his exposure to the master trainer Tom Smith, prepared him for a successful career. "Wild Horse" became one of the leading trainers in California. The Southern California racing circuit is considered one of the most competitive in the world, but Jones set a record by becoming the leading trainer at Del Mar for seven straight years, beginning in 1960. The Farrell Jones Award is annually given to the top trainer at Del Mar Race Course. The fact that the award is named for him is an indication of the esteem in which Jones is held.

Jones retired from training in 1980, but continues to make his presence felt in the world of the Thoroughbred horse. He operates the Farrell W. Jones Thoroughbred Farm in Hemet, California. This twenty-acre facility is devoted entirely to racehorse rehabilitation. His expertise as a trainer has made his facility a popular lay-up farm for horses needing the rest and rehabilitation that will allow them to return as competitors.

HUBERT JONES: When S. C. "Curley" Jones began working

on Ridgewood Ranch, he brought his two children with him. "Curley" began as a ranch hand and cowboy, but soon became a foreman on Ridgewood. His son, a young teenager, was Hubert Jones. He and his sisters, Laverne and Betty, grew up enjoying the beauty of Ridgewood and the horses that brought it fame.

Hubert began riding almost as soon as he began walking. By the age of six he began showing horses and showed hunters and jumpers for several years. As rewarding as this was, his dream was to become a jockey. His horsemanship, coupled with his small stature did not go unnoticed by Charles Howard and he soon put Hubert under contract to ride for him. The Howard's became his legal guardians and arranged to have Tom Smith take him under his wing. At Agua Caliente, on August 15, 1943, he rode in his first race. The ride was a winning one and it was on a horse named Civil Code. Civil Code was imported from Great Britain when Howard purchased his dam, Goldrim. He was a very fast horse, a Stakes winner of twenty-eight races, setting a track record for five and one-half furlongs at Hollywood Park.

Hubert's sister, Laverne (Jones) Booth, described his career. "Within a few months he was one of the leading riders on the West Coast. On June 11, 1944 at Agua Caliente he rode eight winners in one day, setting a new world's record (recorded in the Guinness Book of World Records). In 1945 he was winning Handicap races in Mexico City, Santa Anita and Hollywood Park, including the winning of the Haggin Stakes on Sea Swallow, one of Seabiscuit's best foals. Hubert was then about to be drafted into the armed forces as World War II was winding down, so he enlisted in the Navy and served 12 months. Returning to racing in 1946, Jones was now 2 inches taller and he was not able to keep his weight below 120 pounds. He rode, and won, his last race at Bay Meadows on November 20, 1946."

Jones, no relation to Farrell Jones, continued his life-long career with racehorses by serving as a racing steward at the major tracks in California, until his retirement. Hubert was diagnosed with a brain tumor in 1996 and died shortly after the discovery. His sister Laverne said, "If he was still with us I know he would enjoy being involved with this resurrection of Charley Howard and Seabiscuit."

Seabiscuit "flies" in a workout, "piloted" by George Woolf.
Photo courtesy of The Seabiscuit Heritage Foundation

THE COUGAR

4

John (Red) Pollard was born and raised in Edmonton, Alberta, Canada.

The year of his birth was 1909. He was given the nickname "Red" for obvious reasons, but he preferred to be called "Cougar." That was the nom de ring he gave himself during his days as a prizefighter. Such a name was supposed to intimidate and strike fear into the hearts of his competitors. Red, according to his nephew, John C. Pollard, was not the failed boxer as depicted in the movie. He said, "Red's daughter Norah, has a box full of medals won by him."

All three of the Pollard brothers were boxers. The youngest brother, Bill, was the most successful fighter of the trio. He was of Golden Gloves and Olympic quality and was heading for the Olympics when he suffered a career ending injury in the ring.

The Edmonton area, in the early 1900's, was in the Western Canadian wilderness. His father had been a successful businessman, manufacturing bricks. However, in 1924 a flood destroyed his factory and the family experienced financial problems. Red was the second oldest of the seven siblings and the oldest of the three boys. He had a talent for riding horses. According to his nephew John, his family did not abandon Red. He ran away to follow his dream of becoming a successful jockey. At five feet seven inches, he was tall for a jockey, but did manage to obtain mounts. Obtaining winning mounts, he found, was an entirely different thing.

Red had always been athletic and combined that with a thirst for literary knowledge. Ralph Waldo Emerson and William Shakespeare were his favorite authors. An interesting fact, related by his nephew, was that he was also a history buff and could recall historical facts readily and relate them as though he had been there when they happened.

Pollard was riding at the bush tracks in Montana. In 1925, in Butte, Montana, his guardian had abandoned him and Red was living on his own at the age of sixteen. His best friends and constant companions were his books. He rode for two years before he finally won an official race. He rode for another five years before he won a stakes race. By that time he was riding at Caliente Race Track in Mexico and won the Agua Caliente Derby.

In 1927, Pollard was "sold" to an owner named Freddie Johnson. At that time, apprentice jockeys were considered marketable property. Johnson's trainer, Russ McGirr, found that Red had a unique ability. Having lived a troubled life, Red had come to understand that trading kindness for the whip was the best method of getting a troubled horse to run for him.

He led the life of a racetrack gypsy, riding in Western Canada, Montana, Nebraska, California, Mexico and on rare occasions at Woodbine, in Eastern Canada. It was there, in 1933, that he had what he undoubtedly considered a major win when he rode the Dis Donc horse, Dis Dat, to victory in the

King Edward Gold Cup Handicap. The depression era purse was a paltry twelve hundred dollars.

Wins, however, were more the exception than the rule. While Red lacked a respectable winning percentage, the one thing he never lacked was courage. His loss of vision in his right eye affected his depth perception. Jockeys did not wear goggles, in those days, and a clod of dirt, kicked up by a horse in front of his mount, had caused the loss. It was not, as depicted in the movie, a boxing injury. Although he could see little to his right, he never backed away from charging for a narrow opening between horses. His loss of vision remained his secret throughout his career. Disclosing the problem would have resulted in the rescinding of his license to ride.

By 1936, Pollard's career, such as it was, was fading. He was struggling for mounts at Thistledown racetrack in Ohio, winning a race every couple of weeks. He and his agent decided to try their luck at a track north of there. When they reached Detroit, they suffered a car accident and found themselves stranded with a broken down car, twenty-seven cents in cash, a sugar cube and a bottle of cheap whiskey that Pollard referred to as bow-wow wine. They headed for the racetrack at the Detroit Fairgrounds. It was here that Pollard's life took a turn for the better. By chance, he met Tom Smith, who happened to be looking for a jockey.

Laura Hillenbrand, in a *Thoroughbred Times* article, stated, "He was statistically one of the sport's worst riders. But at the Detroit Fair Grounds that day, he had the one extraordinary stroke of luck in his extraordinarily unlucky life. He gave his sugar cube to a battered racehorse named Seabiscuit, a kindred soul, and won the job as the horse's rider. For Red, it would be the lone success in a career punctuated by incomprehensible hardship." Smith was known for his insistence that his staff must treat his horses with kindness and when he saw this attribute in Red, he immediately hired him. Talk about fate. A chance accident at the right time and the right place and the Seabiscuit crew was beginning to take form. On August 22, 1936, Seabiscuit made his first start in the Howard colors and The Cougar was aboard. By the end of September, the pair had made five starts in Detroit and had won two Stakes. The Seabiscuit legend was on the road to fame and Pollard was attached firmly to its coat tails.

During Pollard's hospitalization and recuperation from his 1939 injuries, he had the good fortune to meet Agnes Conlon. She was his nurse while he was in the Frank R. Howard Memorial Hospital in Willits, California. The hospital, named for Howard's deceased son, is located a short distance from Ridgewood Ranch. Agnes came from a family from the prestigious Back Bay neighborhood in Boston and was engaged to marry a doctor. Red turned on his Irish charm and captivated a lovely young woman whose background and social status would ordinarily have been unreachable by a down and out jockey. They were married that spring. The wedding was planned by Marcela and financed by The Howards.

Over sixty-five years later an occurrence that almost seems to be too strange to be anything other than fiction, happened. At the time I was interviewing John Pollard, who is Red's nephew, he was in need of a job. He was living in southern California and, by chance, read an advertisement for a position for which he was qualified. It was for a Medical Technologist and it was at the Frank R. Howard Memorial Hospital in Willits. Not only did he secure the position, but he discovered that the laboratory, in which he was to work, was the converted hospital room which Red Pollard had occupied.

Few expected Pollard to be capable of returning to his riding career on Seabiscuit, but Red was determined to do so. By the spring of 1940, the two former cripples made their famous comeback. The "Four good legs between them" had become six.

Shortly after Seabiscuit's Santa Anita Handicap win, and subsequent retirement, Agnes gave birth to their daughter Norah. A son, John, was to follow a few years later. Norah was named for one of Red's sisters and John for his father and his grandfather. This is additional evidence that there were no hard feelings or resentment for his allegedly having been abandoned. Norah's passion for literature, she has a Masters degree in English literature, was undoubtedly influenced by her father. She is an award winning poet and the author of "Leaning In," a book of poems, many which are written about her father. The book, published by Antrim House Books, received high acclaim. Norah has read her work widely at venues such as Yale University.

Upon Seabiscuit's retirement, Pollard decided to give his battered body a similar fate. He began training Thoroughbreds, but soon went back to his first love, riding. Two years later he attempted to serve his country by enlisting in the Armed Forces. He was rejected by all three services. His many injuries kept him from passing the physicals. His riding career plummeted and once again he hustled for rides at the bush tracks. He rode at Narragansett, the track at which Seabiscuit won his first race and his first stakes race. He remained there until the track closed down and was leveled by bulldozers.

Agnes was cut from a much finer cloth than Pollard and the nomadic lifestyle of a less than successful jockey was not one in which she could live. The couple bought a cottage in Pawtucket, Rhode Island and Agnes remained there to raise her children. Pollard continued his nomadic career, such as it was, and the couple remained married until their deaths.

Pollard had long since become re-acquainted with his birth family. He kept in close contact with them and visited Edmonton every couple of years to be with his family. He was also very close with his brother Bill. The latter lived in Southern California at the time that Red was riding Seabiscuit and the two would often visit. John said that "Uncle Red, drove me to the DMV to get my first driver's license when I was sixteen." The entire Pollard family was very fond of Red and his lovely wife Agnes and Bill was Red's Best Man when he married Agnes.

Red's fame was to be short lived and due only to the remarkable affinity that he and Seabiscuit had for each other. When Seabiscuit's career ended in 1940, Pollard's career began to slip into anonymity. By 1955, thirty years after his first ride, Pollard retired from the saddle. His riding career had declined and he was again riding bad horses at the "bush" tracks, as he had at the beginning of his career. Time, age and injuries had finally taken their toll to the extent that Red was no longer able to convince trainers to hire him to ride their horses.

His love for the racetrack life overpowered his love for family. He remained in racing until he could physically no longer care for himself. He had fallen from his celebrity status during the Seabiscuit days, to eking out a living as a jockey's valet, polishing boots and doing whatever it took to remain on the fringes of racing.

In 1980, Agnes was diagnosed with cancer and Pollard was living in a nursing home, placed there by their children. By another strange coincidence, the nursing home had been built on the old Narragansett Park site. Pollard would finish his life on a racetrack, or at least on what had once been one. His wife was with him when his body, battered by injuries and abuse, finally gave out. It was early in 1981. Agnes followed him in death two weeks later.

Pollard was inducted into racings Hall of Fame in 1982, an honor that even The Cougar would have thought unlikely.

Pollard on his favorite mount, Seabiscuit.
Photo courtesy of The Seabiscuit Heritage Foundation

A 1960 photo of a retired Red Pollard (center) with Patrol judge Hubert S. Jones (left) and trainer Farrell Jones (right). All three had been contract riders for Charles S. Howard.
Photo courtesy of The Jones Family Archives

Best Buddies, The "Biscuit" and "Red."
Photo courtesy of The Seabiscuit Heritage Foundation

THE "BUG BOYS"

ED POLLARD, also known, to his delight, as "The Cougar" was known for his hot temper, which flared at the proverbial drop of a hat. His early years of struggle and strife are well described in Hillenbrand's bestseller. As an aspiring jockey, riding on the bush tracks during the early 1920's, he suffered abuse and was forced to take life-threatening risks if he wanted to get mounts. In order to make a comparison with Pollard's experiences and those of jockeys in later years, this writer interviewed two other jockeys who began their careers on similar bush tracks. Hopefully, these interviews would show an improvement in attitudes and regulatory matters when it came to protecting the riders.

Apprentice riders have been dubbed with the name "Bug Boys." The horses they ride are given a weight consideration due to the rider's lack of experience. This is an incentive for trainers to give the apprentice jockey a chance to ride while allowing their horses to carry less weight. An asterisk (*), which resembles a bug, is inserted next to their name, signifying that the jockey is an apprentice, or "Bug Boy."

Pollard was born in 1909 and began pursuing his dream of becoming a jockey at the age of fifteen. The other two jockeys were born in 1929 and 1953. I felt that the range in time of twenty and twenty four years might indicate changes. Or they might not.

CLARENCE "CORK" TYE was born on March 25, 1929 in Greeley, Colorado. He began riding saddle horses as a young boy and developed a life-long love for horses. At that time there was a half-mile track in Greeley and Tye, at the age of fourteen, was approached about becoming an exercise boy. He was in Jr. High School at the time and would go to the track each morning before school, working as many horses as time permitted. There was no formal training. His training consisted of instructions from other exercise riders who were also galloping horses.

A year or so later, as Tye put it: "Some fool thought that I was ready for my first race." It was a match race, but not quite the quality of the Seabiscuit/War Admiral match. Tye lost the match, but won on his second mount later in the same day. Jocks always remember their first winner. This one was a seven-year-old mare, Jack's Rose by Jack Collins, who was nearing the end of her racing career. Tye rode her to her fourth win in forty-seven career starts. After retirement, she produced two foals, both winners.

Tye experienced many of the same problems that Pollard did. Rough riding was as common a practice on the bush tracks in the forties as it was in the twenties. Jockeys continued to use their bat (a whip) on other riders and took their competitors wide on the turns, making them lose many lengths during the course of the race. This practice also ran the risk of putting the horse and jockey over the outside rail of the track, not a rare occurrence on the little half mile ovals. The turns were so sharp that many horses had a problem in navigating them. "Cork" said that he was "never dumped, in a race, and actually never witnessed it." He said that most of the rough riding tactics were disguised as unintentional and that most of the jockeys "had a little man complex and were quick to start a fight over antics in a race." This is sometimes referred to as the "Bantam Rooster" attitude.

Tye said that, by the time he could ride well enough to be competitive, he was having a weight problem and that he "quit riding when he got tired of taking Benzedrine." He felt, regarding his weight problem, "that it was insanity to fight it." "Cork" rode for about four years, mostly on the "bush tracks" in Colorado and South Dakota. He ended his riding career at Centennial Park in Colorado, in 1949. After retiring as a rider, he became a jockey's agent for a period of time, but wisely decided to continue his education and graduated from Sacramento State College in 1957 with a teaching credential. He taught sixth grade for a year, Junior High for two years and moved up to the High School level where he taught mathematics and physical education in Napa, California. He also coached baseball for about twenty-five years until his retirement. He then moved back to his former location in Colorado where he currently owns and manages a large cutting horse facility and is the Syndicate Manager for several prominent Quarter Horse stallions.

One major factor, which has a profound effect on the success and survival of young jockeys, has changed little through the decades. Journeymen jockeys will usually refuse to take a mount that they consider to be ill mannered or unsound and a risk for them to ride. An apprentice, if he wants to get mounts, will take just about anything offered. Tye commented that he "was surprised that a lot of apprentice riders aren't injured more than they are." He recalled riding a horse at Hot Springs, South Dakota that had been ruled off in Michigan for "flipping in the gate." The decision to rule him off, for the safety of the riders, should have been honored when he journeyed west from Michigan, but the ruling was ignored. The change of locales did nothing to improve his manners and he continued his aberrant behavior. Fortunately, Tye escaped injury. Many do not.

In retrospect, it appears that conditions for apprentice riders, on the backstretch of the bush tracks, improved during the twenty years between the times that Pollard and Tye began riding, but not to a substantial degree. Perhaps the difference was in the familial ties of the riders. Pollard was pretty much abandoned and on his own without the support of his family, while Tye had a strong family affiliation to protect him. This is not to say that his family approved his choice of going to the racetrack. They were understandably concerned about the influence that the rough, and sometimes wild, environment may have on their young son. Despite their objections Tye elected to become a jockey. Fortunately, strong family influences were present for Tye. Unfortunately, they were lacking for Pollard.

TOM "CUTBANK" CHAPMAN entered the world on October 11, 1953. He was born in Choteau, Montana, which is a small town about fifty miles northwest of his hometown of Great Falls in that State. He grew up in Cutbank, Montana and was given that town's name as his nickname by Gene Peterson, who was the Assistant Clerk of the Scales at Bay Meadows Race Track in San Mateo, California. Tom said that he had several other nicknames and that he "would answer to almost anything."

Tom's interests, during his formative years were varied. He had always been interested in art, but he temporarily gave that up to pursue a sports career. While in high school, he was The Montana State Champion wrestler in the 101-pound class. He said that he had always been small and athletic and some of his friends, who had horses, suggested that he consider becoming a jockey. After graduating from high school Tom enrolled in college, but decided to postpone his education and try his luck at riding. He went to work for a Quarter Horse trainer and he said "I worked for him for a week and decided that was the path I wanted to take. You get to work outside, you get to work with magnificent animals and the potential for making a good living was there."

At this point, Tom's choices were quite different from those of Pollard and Tye. Tom galloped horses around the Fairs and bush tracks in Montana for a few months and made the decision to head for Southern California. He realized that he was going to have to start at the bottom, wherever he started, so he may as well start where the opportunities for advancement were better.

Rex Ellsworth, breeder/owner of the great champion Swaps, had established a jockey school in Chino, California. Chapman was accepted and enrolled in the school. He "learned a lot from the ground up" and worked for Ellsworth and his partner, trainer Mich Tenny, for over two years. At that point he decided to go out on his own and began to freelance at Santa Anita racetrack. His first ride in a race was at Santa Anita. Major trainer, Henry Moreno, became a mentor to Tom and he gave the apprentice rider his first mount. She was a mare named Zulla Road, a Stakes Placed daughter of Quadrangle. She ran fourth on that day. On April 20, 1977, twenty-three year old Tom Chapman won the first race of what was to become a very successful career. The horse, a son of Sailor, was named Lead Line. When asked who was most influential in his development as a rider, Tom gave credit to one of the leading jockeys of the time, Fernando Toro. He also studied Bill Shoemakers' riding. He said, "The Shoe could really get a lot of run out of a horse without looking like he was doing anything."

When questioned about any experiences that he had which were similar to the problems that Red Pollard experienced in his early days of riding, he felt that things had changed a great deal from that time. He feels that it became much safer for jockeys since cameras were installed to record the races. There is little that can escape the eye of the camera and any willfully malicious act can result in the suspension of the perpetrator. Tom said that there were scores of times when he was in danger of being injured, but rarely was it intentional.

As for problems with other jockeys or trainers he said that he is so easy going that most people can get along with him and if he didn't get along with someone, he just stayed away from them. That's not to say that he didn't have to overcome problems. As with "Cork" Tye, being small resulted in getting picked on a lot. He said that he "had a lot of fights. Most of them were verbal, but some were physical. I ended up by polishing a pretty sharp wit, which I was able to use later on as a jockey. I found out that you could say almost anything to anybody if you said it with respect and in a humorous way." When he first began riding in Northern California, he said he got into a couple of scuffles in the "Jocks' room," but when the stewards began suspending riders for their actions, the fighting ceased.

One of Tom's best mounts was the great Irish mare Sangue, winner of over one and one quarter million dollars. He also rode Moment to Buy and the winner of $1,420,550 Slew of Damascus.

Chapman was naturally small, so he had no real problem with his weight. He said that he had some weight problems when he first started out, but they were due to poor eating habits. He was able to control his weight without using any extreme measures. His retirement had nothing to do with a weight problem. He retired in 1996 " in order to spend more time with my wife and kids and I also wanted to go out while I was still at the top of my game. Besides, I had another career (painting) to fall back on and that made it a lot easier."

In retrospect it would appear that the trials and tribulations of the more recent jockeys are not nearly as traumatic as they were when Red Pollard began riding. Another thing to consider is the difference in the attitude exhibited by Tye and Chapman as compared with Pollard's method of dealing with antagonists. Tye and Chapman learned to resolve their problems verbally, by using their wits. Pollard, on the other hand, simply seemed to paint a target on his chest and defy anyone to take dead aim on it. The close observation of the riders, aided by cameras, has definitely resulted in better-regulated riding and less danger to life and limb. That's not to say that danger doesn't exist. Racing is still the only sport where an ambulance follows immediately behind the participants.

Tom Chapman, a triple threat man. A champion wrestler, a leading jockey and an outstanding artist.
Photo courtesy of *The California Thoroughbred* magazine

CHARLES AND MARCELA

*I*t was 1877 when Charles Howard was born in Marietta, Georgia. He spent his youth as a New Yorker, but preferred the open spaces of the west. His preferences for the back of a horse would be replaced by his love for the automobile and he would eventually trade in his reins for a steering wheel. But, while still in his teen years he enlisted in the cavalry. The Spanish American War had begun on April 25, 1898 and young Charles longed for the excitement and adventure of charging up San Juan Hill with Teddy Roosevelt. His time in the cavalry would hone his horsemanship skills, but his dream of battle in Cuba was not to be. His only battle was with dysentery at Camp Wheeler in Alabama. The war proved to be a brief one and a Treaty of Peace was signed on December 10 the same year it started. Despite the fact that he did not charge up San Juan Hill, or any other hill, he acquired the nickname of Rough Rider Charlie.

Howard's move from horses to automobiles was a gradual one. In the intervening years he became a skilled bicycle repairman in New York City. It was there that he married his first wife, Fannie May. They had two sons. However the young father was not cut out for the hectic life of an eastern city. It smothered him and he decided to answer the call of the west. At the age of twenty-six, in 1903, he boarded a train for San Francisco. As the story goes, he arrived at "The City by the Golden Gate" with twenty-one cents in his pocket and a promise to his young family to send for them as soon as his finances improved. Kittridge Collins, Howard's great-grandson, was quoted in the San Francisco Chronicle as saying, "The truth is he came from money, but his father was itinerant, oft married and generally shady. The father had been a real scoundrel."

Howard and a partner, Charles Barry, amassed enough capital to begin a bicycle repair shop in San Francisco. Within two years they decided that the automobile was the sign of the future. They agreed to get into the car dealership business, but did not agree as to which of the numerous makes would succeed. Howard thought the Buick was the way to go. Barry was certain that the Willis Knight would prove the more popular. Howard was right. The two went their separate ways and Howard headed for Detroit to convince Billy Durant that he was the right person to present the Buick to the future motorists in San Francisco.

The first twenty-eight Buicks were built in 1903. By the time Howard returned to San Francisco with his first three cars, there were over two thousand Buicks on the road and Charles was soon to become the sole distributor for the eight western states.

Several months later he was still in possession of the three cars. Not an earth shattering success story. In April of 1906 an earth-shattering event did occur in the form of the great San Francisco earthquake and fire. Rescue operations bogged down. Horse drawn wagons were useless. The horses were terrified of the fires and the explosions from gas mains and the dynamite being detonated to halt the blaze. Howard, always one to turn disaster into success, put his three Buicks into service. They rescued the injured and delivered the dynamite to the front lines of the fire. More importantly, to Howard, they convinced the public of the value of the automobile.

Howard, ever the master salesman, made certain that his cars continued to be in the public's eye. He inaugurated car races, led road tours and thought up every possible stunt to impress buyers with the idea of trading in their horse and buggy for a gas buggy. He was in the car business. Within a year he had sold eighty-five new Buick White Streaks for the huge price of $1,000 each. He was soon shipping trainloads of cars to San Francisco. By 1912 he filled seventy-five train cars with 375 new Buicks. He made certain that the massive shipment got the publicity it deserved and the public turned out for the spectacle when they arrived. Howard became one of America's wealthiest men. According to Ridgewood resident Tracy Livingston, in 1917 Howard loaned cash deficient General Motors three million dollars. In return he got "a piece of the action of every car General Motors sold."

Success followed success for the entrepreneur and Charles and his family, who had long since joined him, became socially prominent San Franciscans. All he needed to fulfill his western dreams was a ranch on which to relax far from the pressure of business. In 1921 he found his ranch in Sonoma County, 135 miles north of San Francisco. Located near the town of Willits, it spread over 16,000 acres of valley and mountains. Its beauty was breath taking. Giant redwood trees surrounded streams and lakes and the lush natural pastures were just begging to be filled with cattle and eventually with Thoroughbred horses. This was the now famous Ridgewood Ranch.

Horses, however, were the last things Howard planned. He was now the largest automobile dealer in the world and according to legend said, "I wouldn't give five dollars for the best horse in the country." He would soon change his mind. Success brought a luxurious lifestyle. He belonged to numerous prestigious golf clubs and kept his 163-foot yacht at San Francisco's St. Francis Yacht Club. A far cry from the three unsold cars in his first year of business, by the 1940's he was marketing up to 30,000 cars a year.

Sadly, all was not wine and roses for the Howard family. Frankie was the third of four sons born to Charles and Fannie Mae. He was born in California in 1911 and, at the age of fifteen was tragically killed in an accident on Ridgewood. He and two neighboring boys decided to go fishing in a lake on the ranch. Frankie was driving and got too close to the edge of a bank. The pick-up truck rolled down the bank, landing on Frankie. The other boys suffered only minor injuries when thrown clear of the wreckage. There was no local hospital and it was thought that, had there been one, young Frankie might have been saved. Howard's good friend, Dr. Babcock, convinced him to build and endow a hospital in near-by Willits. In 1928 it was dedicated and The Frank R. Howard Memorial Hospital continues to be considered one of the finest small hospitals in the country.

The family was devastated and the couple grew apart. Both were suffering a deep depression. The tragedy finally caused their marriage to end in divorce. Famed divorce lawyer Edmond Herrscher successfully won a $2.5 million settlement for Fannie May as well as her hand in marriage.

Their oldest son, Lin Howard had married Anita Zabala. She and her sister, Marcela, had grown up on a small ranch near Salinas, California and were descendants of one of California's first Spanish families. Salinas is a farming area about 100 miles south of San Francisco. Lin invited his father to attend the Salinas Rodeo and his fate was sealed. Also attending was Marcela, a beautiful local actress and experienced horsewoman. Crowned "Lettuce Queen" at a local pageant, Marcela's beauty was much more than skin deep. She had been educated in a convent and her beauty, combined with a calm and caring demeanor, immediately captivated the attention of Charles Howard. Anita was "expecting" and Marcela was staying at Lin's home, in order to help the family. Charles increased his visits to his son's home and finally asked the twenty-five year old beauty to become his wife. He was fifty-two and the May-December marriage was looked upon by many with raised eyebrows. Boy, were they wrong. It was a marriage made in heaven. Marcela was exactly what Howard needed to bring him out of the doldrums.

To quote from the book *Seabiscuit–an American Legend*, by Laura Hillenbrand: "In Marcela, Howard found his perfect compliment. Like him, she was deeply empathetic. Suddenly elevated into the world of the rich, she moved with an easy, charming propriety, yet had the rare grace and aplomb to make her frequent departures from convention seem amusing instead of scandalous. She dazzled the society writers. At golf, she packed such a wallop that she swung from the men's tee. In 1935, when Charles organized a five-month African safari, Marcela eagerly enlisted in the adventure. In a world when women's roles were still highly traditional, Marcela's trip was the talk of the town, prompting the San Francisco Examiner to feature daily reports on her exploits in the jungle. When a lion charged their party, it was Marcela who leveled her gun and coolly shot the animal. And when she found a tiny orphaned blue monkey, she smuggled him back to New York in a hat box." The Howard family presented the gun, which shot the lion, to Laura Hillenbrand.

Marcela was a charming young lady who was suddenly thrust into the spotlight of Howard's glamorous world. At least outwardly, it didn't faze her. Her calm, empathetic attitude captivated everyone she met. She became a second mother to Howard's children and was greatly beloved by Howard's friends and employees and especially the residents of the Willits area. Howard's children, and eventually his grandchildren, called their stepmother Auntie Mar. I have interviewed many people who knew her and all consider her to be one of the most caring and down to earth people they have ever met. No wonder Howard fell in love with her.

The children of the Ridgewood employees benefited from Marcela's special interest in them. She would often buy them clothing, made certain that they had comfortable beds and loaned them a child's saddle when she saw them riding bareback. Laverne Booth, daughter of ranch foreman "Curly " Jones, was one of those children fortunate enough to spend eight years of her youth on Ridgewood. She recalled that when Mrs. Howard saw the three girls, Laverne and Betty Jones and Jani Griffith Buron, "wading in the creek near our house, she invited us to swim in their big pool whenever we wanted to, as long as they weren't using the pool. We spent many hours there on hot summer days."

The couple began attending the races, in Tijuana, Mexico and the cycle, for Howard, had come full circle. He had gone from horses to bicycles to automobiles and now was returning to horses. The couple decided to get involved in horse racing. Howard, considered the wealthiest man west of the Mississippi, could have plunged into the Thoroughbred world in high fashion. He began on a small scale and eventually hired Tom Smith as his trainer. He could have had any of the leading trainers, but saw something in Smith that nobody else had seen. Not only did Smith have the knowledge and talent, but also he had integrity. This was an important factor to Howard.

Next came Seabiscuit and the rest of the story is history and covered in other chapters of this book.

Seabiscuit concluded his racing career with a victory in the Santa Anita Handicap, becoming the world's leading money-winning racehorse.

Howard began building the facilities that would make Ridgewood Ranch one of the best-equipped farms in the west. He built not one, but two twenty-two stall mare barns. The four-stall stallion barn was nearly identical to the barn that housed Seabiscuit's grandsire, Man O' War. The ranch was equipped with the latest in security systems. A night watchman patrolled the farm and punched in at each location to show the time he had been there. This was shortly after the famous Lindbergh baby kidnapping and Howard was determined to protect his family as well as his livestock.

The next great tragedy in Howard's life was the loss of his beloved Seabiscuit. Again, Marcela was involved. It was she who gave the devastating news of his death to Howard and it was she who consoled him. It must have seemed like the end of an era for the Howards, but it just sharpened Howard's competitive spirit and he was determined to replenish his racing stable with other championship prospects.

Howard searched for and bought, outstanding prospects from any country having world-class racing. He often purchased proven runners, hoping that they would repeat their quality, and perhaps improve upon it, for him. Some were successful and others were not. Fair Truckle, an Irish Stakes Winner prior to his importation by Howard proved to be a major sprinter in the United States. At Golden Gate Fields, in northern California, he set a new world record, for six furlongs. He blazed the distance in 1:08 2/5. He also equaled the track record at Hollywood Park at the same distance. At stud he sired a very respectable 10% Stakes Winners from foals. He can be found in the pedigree of many high class racing Quarter Horses, but his blood did not make a major impact on the Thoroughbred breed.

In 1946 Howard imported two sons of the promising young stallion Nasrullah. He was principally interested in Nathoo who had won four major races in England and Ireland, including the Irish Derby. However, Nathoo was unable to contribute to the Howard stable in the United States, running seventh in Belmont Park's Gold Cup. This was to be his only start for his new stable.

As so often happens, the horse which was considered to be inferior to Nathoo, saved the day. This was the great Noor. It wasn't that he was unsuccessful in England. He was a very accomplished horse, being a Stakes Winner at two and three and running third in the English Derby at Epsom. Nathoo was simply considered to be superior. It had been reported, in the Thoroughbred of California magazine that Howard "had to take Noor to get him." (Nathoo).

Noor was a big, powerful horse with great conformation and presence. He placed in three stakes at the age of four and was considered to be a threat whenever he appeared under silks. At five he was a sensation. He won The Santa Anita Handicap, Hollywood Gold Cup, Golden Gate Handicap, American Handicap, San Juan Capistrano Handicap and the Forty-niners Handicap He placed in four others, set three new track records and two world records. The 1950 racing season became famous for the great rivalry between Citation and Noor. The Santa Anita Handicap saw the two meet, with Citation being assigned 132 pounds and Noor 109. The disparity was too much for the great Citation and Noor won, setting a new track record for the mile and a quarter.

Their next meeting was to be the San Juan Capistrano Stakes. Citation would drop two pounds and Noor would pick up eight. The ten-pound difference did not change the result. The two champions raced head and head the length of the stretch with Noor proving victorious by a nose at the trying distance of a mile and three quarters. In this race, Noor not only set another new track record, but a world record as well. Their next encounter was at Golden Gate fields in the mile and a furlong Forty-niners Handicap. Again, the weights were adjusted. Noor was increased to 123 pounds, while Citation dropped to 128. After a thrilling stretch duel, Noor won by a neck in another track record performance.

A week later, for the Golden Gate Handicap, the weights would again be adjusted in Citation's favor. This time Noor would be carrying a pound more than Citation. Noor simply extended his winning streak, this time winning easily by three widening lengths and setting his third world record. The author had the good fortune to be present for this memorable event. It was one of the most impressive races imaginable. In the post parade, Citation stopped and faced the grandstand. He turned his head and surveyed the crowd in its entirety. Seemingly, he was aware that the majority of the huge number of spectators was there for the rare opportunity of seeing a great champion. Then it was Noor's turn to let it be known that Citation was not the only star on the track that day. At precisely the same location that Citation had posed, giving the fans "the look of the eagles," Noor looked at the crowd and kicked up his heels as if to say, "Hey, I'm not chopped liver, take a good look at me."

When the starter's bell rang, California champion On Trust opened up a big lead that he held around the clubhouse turn and down the backstretch. Despite the fact that nearly everybody had bet on either Citation or Noor, the crown roared encouragement for the brilliant home bred. Citation then ranged up along side of On Trust and took over on the far turn. Noor, in the meantime had languished far behind the leaders. At the head of the stretch, Noor lengthened stride and resembling a huge black runaway train, he quickly overpowered his opposition and roared to an easy victory.

The great Noor continued racing through the remainder of the year, after which he was retired. He had never finished worse that third in his twelve starts in 1950 for his trainer Burley Park.

Tragically, Howard had suffered a heart attack and died on June 6 at the age of seventy-three. He was to see only the first two meetings with Citation. The two races at Golden Gate Fields listed Noor as being owned by The Howard Estate. After that he raced for Marcela.

November 27, 1950 saw the dispersal of the breeding stock owned by the Howard Estate. It was held, appropriately, at Santa Anita, the site of so many great victories by the Howard stable. Stallions, mares and yearlings, 109 of them, went under the auctioneers hammer. Noor was retained and entered the stud at the Howard family's San Ysidro Ranch.

Howard had purchased the 147-acre breeding farm in 1937. It was located just north of the Mexican border and was originally built in the 1920's when the only racing, on the west coast, was at nearby Agua Caliente Racetrack. Howard made many improvements on the already well-appointed farm. He constructed a thirty-six stall training barn, a twelve-stall broodmare barn and added a starting gate to the training track. He stood three stallions, including the good sire Exhibit, at the farm and installed fifteen mares. The farm was utilized for lay-ups and the Ridgewood yearlings were shipped to San Ysidro Stock Farm for their early race training. The farm was also used as a retirement home for his ex-racehorses. Jimmy Smith, Tom Smith's son, managed the farm. Noor would later be transferred to Binglin Stock Farm.

Noor was an immediate success as a sire, having several Stakes winners and Stakes placed horses in his first crop. They included the fine mare Nooran, which was out of the Seabiscuit mare Sea Gold. Other Stakes winners, in his first crop of foals, were In Reserve and Prince Noor, as well as Stakes placed Noors Queen. He sired thirteen Stakes winners from his total of 253 foals (5%) and was the most successful sire among the Howard stallions, showing marked quality improvement over the mares to which he was bred. He ended his breeding career at Loma Rica Ranch near the Northern California town of Grass Valley. Renowned horseman Henry Freitas managed the farm for owner Frederick Knoop.

Marcela, widowed at the age of forty-three, had been Howard's loving wife for eighteen years.

In 1952 Marcella married Leslie C. Fenton. He was a British actor and director as well as a decorated Royal Navy officer. In 1976 the couple moved to Montecito, California. Mr. Fenton passed away two years later and Marcela died on March 31, 1987 at the age of eighty-four. She is buried in the Santa Barbara Cemetery, in that California city.

Charles S. Howard in a "playful" mood.
Photo courtesy of The Seabiscuit Heritage Foundation

Charles on Chulo and Marcela riding Seabiscuit are off for a ride in the Ridge-wood hills.
Photo courtesy of The Seabiscuit Heritage Foundation

The Frank R. Howard Memorial Hospital was built by Charles Howard in memory of his son who died in a tragic auto accident on Ridgewood Ranch.
Photo courtesy of The Seabiscuit Heritage Foundation

STRANGER THAN FICTION

There was much about the life and legacy of Seabiscuit that was stranger than fiction and some of it was just that, pure fiction. As with most heroes, Seabiscuit's story grew and was embellished by his fans and his historians.

Descriptions of Seabiscuit, at the time that Howard purchased him, paint him as a violent, neurotic horse that terrorized his handlers. Violent? No! Neurotic? Only to the point of having been over-worked, over-raced and physically abused by the program he was forced to endure. He was exhausted by the routine imposed upon him and was a horse that needed the patient understanding of a Tom Smith. The three-year-old colt had raced a total of thirty-five times as a two year old. Present day two year olds can usually be expected to make four to eight starts during the year. He had just raced his forty-seventh time when he changed ownership in the middle of his three-year-old racing season.

When Smith took over the training responsibility of Seabiscuit, it was during August of 1936 at Saratoga, New York. Farrell Jones, who was to become a successful jockey and a leading trainer, was fourteen years old at the time and was working for the Howard stable exercising Thoroughbreds. He remembers the first time he saw Seabiscuit. On the day he was acquired he was being led over to his new barn and was so quiet and well mannered that Jones thought they had purchased a new saddle horse.

My own recollections, of the time that I knew Seabiscuit, agreed with that description. Seabiscuit was the consummate gentleman. He was a quiet, kind horse with an air of authority and confidence about him. Mr. Howard, then in his sixties, would ride over the vast expanses of Ridgewood Ranch on the champion. A visitor would have mistaken Seabiscuit for a cow pony with his western saddle and tack.

In all fairness to those who depicted him as an aggressive, mean tempered horse, it's very probable that he displayed a cranky disposition when he first came under Smith's care. Most horses, and most people for that matter, do not display their best temperament when totally exhausted.

Seabiscuit was not given much time off after joining the Howard stable. He made his first start in the red and white "Triangle H" silks twelve days later and made eleven more starts before the end of his three year-old career. He steadily increased the quality of races that he was able to win. What caused the improvement he made in class? He came under the magic touch of Smith. He was treated differently than he had been in his former stable. Smith was noted for his insistence that his charges be treated with kindness and as individuals. They were not forced to adhere to a common training regime, instead; the training was altered to fit the need of the individual. The future champ was an unusually intelligent horse and responded positively to the changes.

Another misconception about the two-year old racing career of Seabiscuit is that the colt was a total failure at the onset of his young career. It's a fact that he did not win a race until his eighteenth start. However, it's also a fact that he was second or third in nine of those starts, including a Stakes placement. He finished out his two-year old season with eight additional wins, three seconds and two thirds and five of those wins were in Stakes and Handicaps. By the end of the year he was weighted twenty-eighth on the Experimental Free Handicap. That is an annual evaluation of a horse's accomplishments throughout the year. What this indicates is that Seabiscuit was considered the twenty-eighth best two-year old in the United States in 1935. Not too shabby for a horse who has been dubbed a failure. I know of no owner who wouldn't be proud and pleased to own a colt of that stature. That, of course, is not to say that he was as good at two as he was in later years. He was not a champion at two, but he was by no stretch of the imagination a failure.

It has been reported that Seabiscuit could not run on an "off" track. The fact is that he did prefer a fast track to one that was sloppy or muddy. However, he ran on off tracks a total of six times in his racing career, and was never worse than third. At Belmont Park, September 20, 1938 Seabiscuit ran in the mud in the one and one-half mile Manhattan Handicap. He ran third, carrying 128 pounds. His four competitors were only asked to carry from 100 to 109 ½ pounds over the trying distance and track. Under equal weights, he would have won by half the length of the stretch.

Seabiscuit has been described as being from the wrong side of the tracks. In other words, his bloodlines were plebian. This is far from factual. Seabiscuit was a product of Wheatley Stable. At the time, Wheatley was one of the great breeding farms in Kentucky. His sire, Hard Tack, was bred in the purple, being by the great Man o' War and out of Tea Biscuit who was by the leading broodmare sire Rock Sand. Hard Tack was the successful sire of twelve Stakes Winners. Seabiscuit's dam, Swing on, was by the equally great Whisk Broom 11. Everything in his background indicated that he had the genetic forces to become a successful racehorse.

Then there are those who claim that Seabiscuit was an ugly, plain headed, crooked legged runt who was considered useless by his connections. True, his left front leg was "bucked" over at the knee. This refers to a condition where the knee protrudes forward of the plumb line of the leg. While this may be a cosmetic fault and would rightly be a detriment in a horse show halter class, it is not a soundness problem. In fact, many knowledgeable horsemen consider it a positive feature. As leading trainer Farrell Jones put it: ". . . . horses that are bucked over in the knee are a hell of a lot better than horses that aren't. Horses that are bucked over, that knee extends a little when they hit the ground and that takes the pressure off." As for his "plain" head, one needs only to look at pictures of him to realize the untruth of that statement. He had a classic profile and was wide between his large, expressive eyes. Seabiscuit stood 15 hands two inches tall. While that is smaller than the average Thoroughbred, it can hardly be called a "runt." At any rate, it was big enough to house the heart of a champion.

In other sections of this book, I have discussed the fact that Seabiscuit, contrary to popular opinion, was not a private stallion. He was well advertised as being available to mares owned by others than Charles S. Howard. He was, however, rarely bred to outside mares, but this was due to his being a victim of circumstances. Among those were the six hundred mile distance from Ridgewood Ranch to the concentration of the breeding industry in California, the lack of commercial vans and gas rationing as a result of World War II.

Another unusual feature was the uncanny similarity between Seabiscuit and his grandson Sea Orbit. Sea Orbit, the champion's best descendant, has chapter 12 devoted to him. The two were very similar in conformation. Both were bay in color and considered smaller than average. Seabiscuit was 15 hands two inches and Sea Orbit was 15 hands three inches in height. Most male Thoroughbreds are two or three inches taller. Height was not a factor to either horse. The size of their hearts was the important factor. Also, both horses were extremely intelligent and possessed of kind dispositions and a wonderful attitude.

Most Thoroughbreds are born from February to April. May is not considered a preferred month as they will be competing with horses older than they are. All Thoroughbreds change their age on January first of each year, so a two year old born in January has a distinct advantage over a May foal. Seabiscuit was foaled on May 23, 1933 and Sea Orbit on May 18, 1956. As a matter of fact, War Admiral was also a May foal. So much for that prejudice.

Another coincidence was a track record breaking performance by the two horses. On May 16, 1938, Seabiscuit set a new track record of 1:49 flat for a mile and 1/8 in the Bay Meadows Handicap at Bay Meadows, California. On April 16, 1960, his grandson, Sea Orbit set a new track record, for a mile and 1/8 in 1:47 flat in the Bay Meadows Handicap at the same track.

Both horses concluded their racing careers with Stakes wins at Santa Anita Race Track when they were seven years of age. They both received standing ovations from the fans. The owners of Seabiscuit and Sea Orbit had announced, prior to their final starts, that "Win, lose or draw" this was to be their final races.

Seabiscuit was considered to be a failure as a sire. Although it's true that he was unable to reproduce his championship quality, he was far from a failure. Statistics prove that he improved the racing quality of the foals that his mates produced, over those that they produced when bred to other sires, by forty percent. This figure is derived by the use of the "Average Earnings Index." (See glossary).

Another unusual and sad fact is that neither Seabiscuit nor Sea Orbit would have enough foals or enough quality mares to be considered a success as sires. Finally, and tragically, both horses would meet untimely deaths at an unusually young age.

Seabiscuit and his kitten friend. A female cat gave birth to several litters of kittens in Seabiscuit's stall. He baby-sat them and always made certain that they were safe from harm.
Photo courtesy of The Seabiscuit Heritage Foundation

THE SILENT ONE

The Native Americans, in his early years, called him "Lone Plainsman." To the rest of the country he became known as "Silent Tom Smith." He was born in Georgia in 1878 and by the age of thirteen he was an experienced horse breaker, making a living at his chosen profession by breaking and training horses for the cavalry. Before reaching his teen years he had ridden in the last of the great cattle drives on the Western frontier. He moved west to Grand Junction, Colorado at the age of twenty-one and in Colorado he took a job as foreman on a cattle ranch. He stayed on for over twenty years, breaking, training and caring for their horses. Tom honed his abilities by breaking and training mustangs. The ranch was sold in 1921 and Tom moved on, continuing his Western migration.

In the 1920's Smith worked for C.B. (Cowboy) Irwin's Wild West Extravaganza and his racing stable. Tom worked as a caretaker for the horses in the Wild West Show. He saw to their needs and patched them up so that they could continue to perform. It was a nomadic life and "The Silent One" must have felt that his talents were not being challenged. That changed when Irwin gave Smith a stable of cheap horses to train and race on the Western "bullring" tracks. At Cheyenne, Wyoming, Smith won an amazing twenty-nine out of thirty races. Irwin, being an astute businessman, sent Smith to the State of Washington, with a better string of horses to train, the following year. In the Northwest, he continued to illustrate his talent for training horses.

Smith's perceptive philosophy was to "Learn your horse. Each one is an individual, and once you penetrate his mind and heart, you can often work wonders with an otherwise intractable beast." He also is quoted as saying that "It's easy to talk to a horse if you understand his language. Horses stay the same from the day they are born until the day they die … they are only changed by the way people treat them." By the early thirties America was in the midst of the great depression. Irwin died and the show closed. The Silent One moved farther west. Smith followed the bullring circuit and worked as a groom, mucking out and sleeping in stalls and hit a low point in his life. He was fifty-five years old and flat broke.

One of his charges was a horse named O'Riley. A bottom level claimer, the horse went lame. Smith, somehow or other, acquired him and his Western trek continued.

In 1934 Smith was living in a stall at Mexico's Agua Caliente Race Track just across the border from Southern California. Fortunately for Tom, he was sharing his living quarters, such as they were, with the future great trainer Noble Threewit. His friendship with Threewit led to an introduction to automobile magnet and horse owner, Charles S. Howard. Threewit was impressed with Smith's ability to care for and improve O'Riley. This was the only horse that Tom was training and Noble recommended that Howard hire him. Howard had an amazing ability to sense integrity, ability and potential in an individual. His instincts were usually correct and were right on target with his estimation of Smith.

In 1936, with the urging of his wife Marcela, Howard was ready to enter the big time in racing. He sent Tom east to purchase a horse that could take him to the top. On June 29, at Suffolk Downs in Massachusetts, Smith discovered a horse that he could purchase for $8,000.00. That was a respectable amount during the depression. His horseman's intuition told him that this colt "had the real stuff" and that he could improve on Seabiscuit's past performance. Smith's philosophy was sound; he considered each horse as an individual. He had the ability to understand a horse and to formulate a program that fit that individual. Seabiscuit responded and history was about to be made.

Smith called upon his knowledge, collected over a lifetime, of liniments and healing remedies. He cured Seabiscuit's aches and pains and calmed his nerves by treating him with kindness and by finding him several animal friends. The most famous of these was the palomino gelding "Pumpkin." Pumpkin would be his constant companion throughout his racing career. A few years after Seabiscuit's retirement, Pumpkin was also retired to Ridgewood Ranch and was stabled in a large paddock near Seabiscuit's barn.

After Seabiscuit's final race, when winning the Santa Anita Handicap made him the world's leading money winner, the champion Seabiscuit was permanently retired to Howard's Ridgewood Ranch.

Tom Smith continued to train for Howard for the next three years. The year prior to Seabiscuit's win in The Santa Anita Handicap; the Howard/Smith combination won the race with the great Argentinean champion, Kayak II who finished second to Seabiscuit the following year. In 1943, two years later, Tom suffered a serious back injury that necessitated a lengthy convalescence. Howard had no choice. He had to hire a new trainer. Howard and Smith parted on good terms.

As much as Smith respected Howard, he didn't hold Red Pollard in much esteem. This is not necessarily a mark against Pollard. Smith had little respect for any jockey. He felt, as do many trainers, that he worked hard getting horses ready to win. In turning over his horse to a jockey, he lost all control and so often a mistake by the rider could ruin all of his work.

After Smith's recovery, he went to work for the cosmetic queen, Elizabeth Graham Arden. Ms. Arden was noted for changing trainers so often that it was difficult to keep track of who was training for her. She insisted that trainers use her cosmetic products on her horses and trainer after trainer hit the unemployment line by refusing to respond to what they considered to be frivolous demands. Unbelievably, what was apparently the original "odd couple" (Tom and Elizabeth) appeared to get along famously. Ms. Arden had great respect for Smiths' ability. She always demanded that her horses be treated with the utmost kindness and that was a trademark of Smith's training methods. She made the statement that "There's something about Tom Smith that gives you confidence." Arden had the financial ability to purchase the top of the market racing prospects and Smith catered to her whims as long as they did no harm to his charges.

In 1945 Tom trained Star Pilot and Beaugay for the Arden stable. They were voted the champion colt and filly of that year. From all appearances the Arden stable, master minded by Smith was set to make racing history.

That year was a banner year for the great trainer. It was also the lowest point in his career. The only black mark in an otherwise unblemished training career took place in 1945. One of his stable hands was observed spraying a nasal decongestant into the nose of one of the stables lesser horses. At that time, New York racing laws banned the use of any medications. Although Smith had not instructed his employee to administer the nasal spray and was, in fact, unaware that it had been used, he was held responsible. Trainers are held responsible for anything dealing with the horses under their care. It was a very controversial decision. Testimony revealed that the horse, Magnific Duel, had received eight squirts of a nasal spray containing ephedrine. This was an amount that, in the testimony of one expert witness, "could not have affected the physical performance of a flea." Magnific Duel, although of regal breeding as all of the Arden horses were, was a disappointment as a racer. He ran 58 times, over a period of six years and earned a dismal $7,905. This was hardly the sort of horse that a leading trainer would risk his career over by administering a banned substance.

Smith had his trainer's license suspended for a year. Actually, it was not suspended, but revoked. Technically, this gave Smith the option to appeal the decision. The case dragged on for a year at which time the length of the suspension was up and he was reinstated. Hardened criminals are afforded a more rapid trial, but Silent Tom suffered, true to his nickname, in silence.

Arden immediately rehired Smith. Her decision was a wise one. He took over the training of his two year old champion and repaid Arden's confidence by leading Star Pilot, following his Kentucky Derby win, into the winners circle at historic Churchill Downs.

On two occasions, Smith was the leading trainer in the United States. He trained a total of 29 stakes winners prior to his 1957 forced retirement, due to a stroke. He lived out his final days in a convalescent hospital, dying later in that year at the age of seventy-seven. Basically forgotten, broke and for the first time in his life, without his beloved horses, the Silent

One was forever silent. Few turned out to mourn this talented trainer, but "Silent" Tom Smith's story did not end with his death. Thanks mainly to Laura Hillenbrand's book, published in 2001, Smith was finally enshrined in the Racing Hall of Fame later that year.

A 1944 picture of Tom Smith with Hubert Jones at Jamaica, New York.
Photo courtesy of The Jones Family Archives

RIDGEWOOD–FROM POMO
TO THE GOLDEN RULE

THE POMO.

The original inhabitants of the area now known as Ridgewood Ranch, Home of Seabiscuit, were The Northern Pomo peoples. It is accepted as a fact that the name "Pomo" was derived from "Poma." This was the name given to a village in the area, by Anthropologists, at the turn of the century (1,900). Actually, the Pomo were comprised of seven different cultural groups, each speaking distinctly different languages. Unfortunately, the language is now extinct. The Northern Pomo, living North of the Gulala River are named The Bokeya. The Gulala River was the border between the Bokeya and the Yokiya tribes of Pomo. The Bokeya resided on the land that is now Ridgewood Ranch.

Indian legend held that a hole in the surrounding mountains allowed an ocean breeze to keep the valley's climate ideal.

In 1700 the population of the Pomo was estimated to be 8,000. By 1852, when the Ridgewood property had its first white resident, the number had dwindled to 4,200 and then to 1,300 by the turn of the century. Various groups, to secure slaves, had subjected the Pomo to RAIDS. Additionally, there were dramatic increases in deaths from diseases such as smallpox. The low point of the population was in 1963 when the number dropped to 1,033, but by 2000 it had increased to 2,400, due to an improvement in living conditions and health care.

The Pomo were a peaceful and creative people who would have found the valley idyllic. Food was plentiful. Deer thrived in the environment and the two year-round streams provided fresh water and fish. The huge oak trees produced ample acorns, which was their favorite food. The Pomo lived a simple life and are noted for their ability to create fine basketry. The Native American tribes of California are famed for their beautiful baskets and the Pomo are considered by many to have been the most skilled of the basket makers. Both men and women made baskets.

During the California gold rush, the State sold off much of the Pomo land to anyone willing to buy it and in later years, with poor representation in a court case, they lost 80,000 acres. Today the Pomo have only fifty acres of tribal land.

CAPTAIN WALKER.

The government of the United States sent Captain Walker to the area, assigning him the task of establishing a government trapping post. Walker retired from the army in the 1850's and became the first white resident of the ranch. He moved in, with his family, and raised cattle. Prior to his arrival the valley had been known as Spring Valley, but it soon became known as Walker Valley.

RENCH ANGLE.

Angle became the second owner of the property. He purchased the ranch in 1859 for an average of $3.25 an acre. The purchase price varied greatly for the seventy-five sale transactions that he completed in order to consolidate the ranch property. Prices reportedly ranged from seventy-eight cents an acre to six dollars and twenty-five cents an acre. He raised sheep at Ridgewood for over fifty years and lived on the property with his wife and fifteen children. Within a two-week period, six of the children died of Diphtheria. There is a small cemetery on the property, where Angle and nine of his children are buried.

MARGARET MAGUIRE.

Rench Angles' widow remarried and in 1892 she sold the fifteen thousand two hundred and thirty-nine acre ranch to Margaret Maguire for seventy-two thousand five hundred dollars. In 1903 Mrs. Maguire sold off portions of the ranch to various interests, including nearly ten thousand acres to William Van Arsdale

WILLIAM VAN ARSDALE.

In 1903, William Van Arsdale became the next owner of Ridgewood and purchased surrounding acreage. An engineer and timber entrepreneur, he was a San Francisco resident and used the ranch as a second home. He grew alfalfa, raised livestock and made major improvements to the property. It was Van Arsdale who gave the property the name of Ridgewood Ranch.

One of his innovative undertakings was the development of the springs on the east side of the ranch. In 1905, he built a 340,000-gallon water-tank and piped the water to the ranch headquarters. One hundred years later it is still functioning. The most unusual feature, for its time, was the installation of a Pelton Water Wheel. The Pelton wheel uses the momentum of a water jet impinging on buckets attached to the periphery of a wheel to produce power. It is a development of the so-called "hurdy gurdy" wheel used in the California gold fields in the 19th century. The water was piped through the waterwheel and generated electricity for the ranch.

Another project was the construction of a beautiful ranch style home and a carriage house. Everything about its construction was done with the finest materials and skilled labor. The home still stands and is in remarkable condition for its age. The house is built in a "U" shape and the entrance is a lovely garden patio enclosed on three sides. The centerpiece of the patio is a massive rock fireplace, one of four in the home. Plans are underway to make necessary repairs and to restore the historical home to its former elegance.

The Carriage House was an elaborately designed building which could house four carriages. During the Howard ownership the structure was converted into apartments for the domestic help and a garage. Undoubtedly it was a discriminatory site. Buicks only! The plan is to reconstruct the original Carriage House. Few are still in existence. Between 1917 and 1921 the ranch changed hands several times.

Charles S. Howard.

In 1921 Charles S Howard purchased the 16,000-acre Ridgewood Ranch. The Howard's were also residents of San Francisco, but spent as much time as possible on the ranch. Howard was a "hands-on" owner who delighted in participating in the daily activities of the ranch. Ridgewood became a much-diversified ranching operation under his ownership. They raised both beef and dairy cattle and had a working dairy on the ranch. Sheep were also raised and large amounts of vegetables and fruit were produced. The excess food, produced on Ridgewood, supplied the hospital built by Howard in memory of his son Frank. Additionally, the local church and other charitable organizations were supplied with fresh produce, milk and meat.

Horses were also bred and raised at Ridgewood. In the beginning horses were raised to work the cattle and for pleasure riding. Workhorses were also raised on the ranch. Eventually Thoroughbred horses became the mainstay of the breeding operation and Ridgewood was developed into a state of the art breeding farm. Numerous stallions graced the property, the most famous being Seabiscuit. Also, siring foals were Kayak II, Mioland, Sabu, Vero, Ajax, Fast and Fair, Sea Sovereign and Fair Truckle.

Howard also imported a miniature Sicilian Jack called Albert. Breeding him to pony mares, he produced very small mules. The mules were used as a team to pull a miniature stagecoach, much to the delight of the children on the ranch and in the area.

Another unusual feature was a herd of rare white deer. Ed Rose, a resident of Ridgewood and a docent for the Seabiscuit Heritage Foundation, supplied information regarding the historical background of the herd. In the early years of the twentieth century a rancher in the small town of Comptche, California received a gift of some white deer from newspaper magnet William Randolph Hearst. The rancher was raising them in pens and, while feeding them one day, during rutting season, was gored by a large buck. He decided that caution was the best part of bravery and turned all but four of them loose. The four were presented to Howard around 1930. Ed States,

"The four deer were released in front of the Howard's house over by the pool and as soon as they left the cage they jumped into the pool." One can only imagine the horrendous task of rescuing four terrified deer from the swimming pool. I have no idea how the job was done, but I'm certain that the ranch cowboys dealt with the problem with their native ingenuity. They have multiplied and thrived and are now about 200 in number (The deer, not the cowboys). The ranch is a sanctuary for the herd and feed is plentiful so they are satisfied to remain within its boundaries.

White deer are uncommon, but not rare. They are a naturally light-colored species and are native to parts of Asia, North Africa and Europe. Their appearance gives one the impression that their natural habitat should be in the far north, perhaps Scandinavia. And that is a correct assumption. One of the largest herds lives in Sarvonia, a region in Finland. They have a natural camouflage against a snowy background, but would be at the mercy of predators in the verdant forests surrounding Ridgewood. Fortunately, they have wisely learned to stay in the valley, where they have more protection from hungry predators and have better grazing. I found it interesting that, while researching the history of the white deer, I discovered an article that described white deer as excellent swimmers. Perhaps that explains why, after their lengthy confinement in small pens, they jumped into the swimming pool.

JEFF AND EDWARD WELCH.

Howard requested that the family, in the event of his death, retain Ridgewood Ranch. However, on the advice of their attorney, the ranch was put on the market. The purchasers, Jeff and Edward Welch, purchased the beautifully appointed ranch for $24.00 per acre. Not interested in breeding horses, they ran cattle on the property. Their primary purpose for purchasing the ranch was their interest in logging and, during the next eleven years, they logged over two hundred and fifty million board feet of timber, mostly by clear cutting. The result left immense areas of the once pristine forest denuded and in dire need of a reforestation plan. The next owner put that plan into effect.

CHRIST'S CHURCH OF THE GOLDEN RULE.

In the mid-1940's, some 850 people founded Christ's Church of the Golden Rule. As stated in the Encyclopedia of American Religions, "The church's creed is The Golden Rule, Therefore all things whatever ye would that men should do to you, do ye even so to them."

In 1962, Christ's Church of the Golden Rule purchased the 16,000-acre Ridgewood Ranch and they currently have owned the property for a longer period of time than has any other, with the exception of the Pomo.

When Ridgewood came under the ownership of The Golden Rule Church Association (GRCA), immediate plans were made, and put into motion, to restore the land. One of their first projects was to plant over ten thousand trees to reforest the clear-cut areas. The members of the church have made it clear that they care deeply about the management and future of their land. As Rose stated: "They have funded the Conservation Easement effort with about 150 thousand in operating capital, donated 7 million dollars worth of developmental rights and spent over 30 thousand on a 100 year Non-industrial Timber Management Plan." Additionally, stream restoration projects have taken place along the Forsythe and Walker creeks. "Over 28,000 redwoods, alders, willows, oaks, dogwoods, bay laurels and maples have been planted along the creeks to create shade important for aquatic life and to stabilize stream banks."

Church members also maintain an extensive organic garden, producing fruit and vegetables for their own use and for sale at the local Farmer's Market. They also donate fresh vegetables and fruit to the local senior center and food bank. The organic garden is not as extensive as it was in 1979. At that time it produced one thousand three hundred seventy-five pounds of carrots, seventeen thousand pounds of tomatoes and nine hundred pounds of onions.

Educational programs are an important part of the church's overall philosophy of sharing the benefits of its land with the public. Some of the activities, hosted by the church, are an annual wildflower walk, a horseback riding project for disabled children, livestock and veterinary science projects for the local 4-H group and historical tours organized by the Willits Chamber of Commerce, The Mendocino County Museum and the Seabiscuit Heritage Foundation. Additionally, the ranch includes "The Golden Rule Mobile Village" which has eighty-seven permanent spaces as well as thirty "overnighter" spaces.

The horseback riding program began in 1993 as a Mendocino County 4-H program. It is called T.R.A.I.L. (Teaching Riding as an Access to Independence and Learning). The program provides assistance because of developmental, social or physical disabilities. Ed Rose, one of the volunteers, said, "Many of our riders are confined to wheelchairs or dependant upon walkers. Their minds and bodies sometimes tell them that they can't do something. But, when they're on the back of a horse, they often discover that they can achieve the very things they thought were impossible." He continues, "In the past twelve years we have had the joy of assisting over 175 children in finding the physical and emotional healing power of therapeutic riding."

The T.R.A.I.L. program has always been offered free to any one in need. Funding comes from local businesses, community organizations, fundraisers and private individuals. They are currently up-grading their facility and plan to expand the program from a seasonal one to a year around program with the addition of a covered arena. The plan is to expand the age group from both ends of the spectrum to include children as young as five and to also add adults to the client base.

It comes as no surprise that the church has received numerous commendations for their land management and public service efforts from several sources, including leaders at the California State Capitol.

Rench Angle with his wife and two of their daughters.
Photo courtesy of The Seabiscuit Heritage Foundation

The Pomo were famed for their basketry.
Photo courtesy of The Seabiscuit Heritage Foundation

Currently being restored, The Howard Mansion was built by William Van Arsdale over one hundred years ago.
Photo courtesy of The Seabiscuit Heritage Foundation

A spring morning at Ridgewood with the white deer in the foreground.
Photo courtesy of Ed Rose and Phaedra Kincaid

The famed white deer of Ridgewood.
Photo courtesy of Ed Rose

THE P08

*I*n 1831, at the age of two, Charles E. Bowles immigrated to New York. He arrived with his parents and six siblings, sailing from Norfolk County, England.

Life on his father's hundred-acre homestead proved to be too dull for young Charles and, at the age of twenty, he and his cousin David headed for the promise of riches in the California gold fields. Wintering in Missouri, they arrived in Sacramento in early 1850. They began their quest on the North Fork of the American River, but soon sought their fortune in other locations in the northern Sierra.

By 1852 Bowles headed for home. Reaching Illinois, he met and married Mary Elizabeth Johnson. They settled in Decatur, and the young family increased to four.

In 1862 the nation was involved in The Civil War and Charles found a way out of the unexciting life in Decatur. On August 13 he enlisted, for a three-year stint, with the 116th Illinois Infantry. He fought with both Grant and Sherman. By the following May Bowles was promoted to First Sergeant, but shortly thereafter he received a severe injury. After a three-month recuperative period he was again with Sherman when they continued their "March to the Sea."

1865 saw him mustered out in Washington, D.C. and he headed for home. Two years of farming was enough to convince Bowles that there had to be something awaiting him that would afford him the excitement for which he craved. He again headed west and the last his family heard from him was in August of 1871 when they received a letter from Silver Bow, Montana. With no further word from him, his family assumed that he was deceased.

For the next four years little is known about his life, but whatever happened during this period changed his destiny.

By the summer of 1875, forty-six year old Charles E. Bowles began a new profession under the assumed name of Black Bart. Self proclaimed as the Poet Laureate of Northern California, he added the suffix Po8 (Poet) to his name and began his lengthy and highly successful career as a stagecoach robber. Not just any stagecoach would do. He specialized in robbing Wells Fargo Stage Coaches. His dislike for the company was reportedly due to a bad experience he had with some of their employees. He was determined to get even with them.

Black Bart's name was not derived from his skin or hair color. He claimed that it was due to his "black heart,' which is highly unlikely. At the time a "Dime Novel" type of adventure story ran as a serial in the Sacramento Union newspaper. A principle character in the series was called the "Black" Bart and his dastardly acts included numerous crimes against the Wells Fargo Co. Almost certainly, Charles came up with the name after reading the stories in the newspaper.

Black Bart's modus operandi was to wait in hiding at a location where the stagecoach would have to slow down. He would leap in front of the stagecoach, his shotgun pointed at the driver and demand that they throw down the strongbox. On the face of it, it appeared no different than that of any other highwayman of the day. However, there were many unusual aspects to the Black Bart method. Most of the highwaymen and bank robbers of that era wanted to be recognized and feared. Becoming notorious was an asset, along with feeding their egos. Bart did everything possible to make himself unrecognizable. He wore a flour sack, with eyeholes, over his head. He also pulled flour sacks up over his boots and wore a full-length linen duster. He was totally covered from head to toe. He made certain that his victims knew who he was by his garb and by the signed poems that he left, but no one knew what he looked like or could identify him by his clothing. Another thing that set him apart from others in his trade was his attitude and his manners. He was polite, but firm. He would quietly say, "Please throw down the strongbox." He used no profanity and would explain to the passengers that he would never take any of their personal effects or their money. He offered them no harm and they had no reason to fear him. It was solely Wells Fargo that had reason to fear Black Bart. Unlike others in his profession, he eschewed riding horses and rarely did so. He was a prodigious hiker and preferred to arrive and leave his crime scenes on foot.

The highwayman would send the coach on its way and proceed to open the box and remove its contents. The strongbox would remain to be retrieved by Wells Fargo, but always with a poem written by the Po8. The first of the poems went as follows:

> *"I've labored long and hard for bread*
> *for honor and for riches*
> *But on my corns too long youve tred*
> *You fine haired sons of bitches*
> *Black Bart*
> *The PO8"*

Legend has it that one of Black Bart's favorite locations, for robbing Wells Fargo, was the top of the pass above the valley that is now the site of Ridgewood Ranch. The historic stagecoach road is now known as U.S. 101 and the pass is still the highest elevation on the nearly fourteen hundred-mile length of the highway from the Mexican to the Canadian borders. By the time that the horses had struggled up the long, steep grade they were exhausted and the coach was an easy prey for the highwayman. This was during the time that Rench Angle was the proprietor of the ranch. After one such robbery, Black Bart emptied the strongbox and hiked down to the Angle ranch house. Travelers were always welcome at the Angle's and this one was no exception. Rench was not at home, but Mrs. Angle and her children joined the traveler in a meal. Always the charming guest, he chatted with them and offered to pay for the meal. It wasn't until much later that Mrs. Angle realized that she had been hostess to the infamous Black Bart.

The P08's career extended from August 3, 1877 to November 3, 1883, a period of six years and three months to the day. He is credited, perhaps "charged" would be a more definitive word, with successfully completing twenty-seven Wells Fargo Stagecoach robberies and his average yearly take was reported to be $6,000. At that time, this amount would allow him to live a very comfortable, if not luxurious, life.

Black Bart planned each escapade with care and made certain that there would be no way that he could be recognized after leaving the crime scene. The flour sacks on his feet would eliminate telltale footprints and his clothing was completely covered by the full-length duster. Also, each line of his poems was written in a different style of handwriting. All went well until his twenty-eighth attempt.

Black Bart's downfall was a handkerchief. The details of his final escapade were widely chronicled at the time. The attempt occurred in Calaveras County in the northern California Sierra Nevada Mountains. It was on the Sonora to Milton stagecoach route that the Po8 met his downfall. There was no one riding "shotgun" on the stage driven by Reason McConnell, so the driver was pleased to give a lift to a teenager who was hunting small game. As the team was struggling up a steep incline, the young hunter, Jimmy Rolleri, decided to disembark in order to do some hunting. He planned to meet the stage on the other side of the hill. As the team neared the top of the grade, Black Bart made his move. He questioned the driver about the lack of a shotgun rider and was told that he was hunting small game. The driver had nailed the strongbox to the floor of the coach, so Bart sent him on his way without the coach and proceeded to use an axe to open the box. It was moments later that McConnell met up with Jimmy and the two returned to the scene of the crime. Bart had just finished opening the strongbox when the pair opened fire on him. Bart, having grabbed the gold and some mail, ran for hiding. The mail, covered with blood, was dropped and the pair realized that they had been successful in wounding the robber.

In his haste to escape, Black Bart was unable to recover his belongings, which had been hidden behind a rock. Nothing was of value in identifying the owner, excepting for a handkerchief used to carry buckshot. The handkerchief had the identifying laundry mark Fx07. James Hume, a Wells Fargo detective, traced the laundry mark to a laundry in San Francisco. The owner was identified as a Mr. Charles E. Bowles who was residing in a hotel on 2nd Street in San Francisco. Hume arrested Bowles who signed the booking slip as "T. Z. Spaulding." Hume's report stated that Black Bart was, "A person of great endurance. Exhibited genuine wit under the most trying circumstances. Extremely proper and polite in behaviour, eschews profanity."

James E. Rice, an employee of the Bank of Italy in San Francisco and a former Agent for Wells Fargo, wrote about the "Remarkable Career of Black Bart" in 1920. In his article he states, "During the many years of service with Wells Fargo & Company and intimate contacts with various types of humanity, one of the most interesting personalities I became familiar with was that of Black Bart." He continues, "The party's real name is said to be C. E. Bolton (The spelling varies from Bowles to Boles to Bolton in various accounts) and he was a resident of [37 second street. Room 40] San Francisco. His practice was to leave his home in the Bay City and take the evening boat for Stockton, arriving in the river town the following morning. Being a wonderful pedestrian, he would usually walk forty miles into the mountains by night time. The next day he would rob a stage and the only evidence he would leave behind would be a "poem" in which there was some humor and occasionally a vulgar line." About his capture and the evidence which led to it, he said, "The handkerchief was taken to San Francisco and after a long search similar marks were found on other linen in a laundry, by Harry Morse, head of the Morse Patrol and Detective Agency of San Francisco. While Morse was in the office of the laundry investigating the marks on the handkerchief, he was told by the proprietor that the gentleman who owned that particular handkerchief was a respected customer, having mining interests in California, and he occasionally was a customer at the laundry. By a rather remarkable coincidence, the "owner" of the linen walked into the building while Morse was there and the detective immediately engaged him in a conversation by stating he understood he was interested in mines. Incidentally, Morse told him that he had some property he would like to submit for his consideration and that he would be glad to show him samples of ore as well as give him other details of the mining prospect. Bart apparently "fell" for what his newly made acquaintance had to offer and agreed to accompany him to the latter's office on Montgomery street. When Bart entered and took in the surroundings, he was satisfied he had been trapped for he threw up his hands and exclaimed, "Gentlemen, I pass."

Bowles was released from San Quentin prison after serving only four of his six sentenced years. The sentence was reduced due to good behavior. Reporters were present when he was released on January 22, 1888 and asked if he planned on robbing any more stagecoaches. "No gentlemen," he smilingly replied, "I'm all through with crime." Another reporter asked if he would write more poetry. He laughed, "Now didn't you hear me say that I am through with crime?"

A short time later Charles E. Bowles, at the age of fifty-eight disappeared. He was last seen on February 28, 1888 in San Francisco's Nevada House. The following day, he left his possessions in his room and he and Black Bart were seen no more. All that remained was their legend. It was up to the historians to determine which of the stories about him were fact and which were fiction.

In 1948, actor Dan Duryea was cast as Charles E. Bowles in the film Black Bart. The film, shot in Technicolor, was also known as "Black Bart, Highwayman."

THE LITTLE *11* BISCUITS

The first small crop of foals, sired by Seabiscuit, was conceived during the time he and Pollard were recuperating on Ridgewood Ranch. It was during the "Four good legs between us" time of their respective careers. That was the appropriate phrase that Laura Hillenbrand coined for The Biscuit and Red Pollard. The seven little Biscuit's were foaled in the spring of 1940, which was the year that Seabiscuit became the world's leading money winner by sweeping to victory in the Santa Anita Handicap.

It was not a very impressive beginning to the champ's stud career. The crop was composed of four colts and three fillies. Seabiscuit's first colt was from the fine mare Illeana. She was probably the best producer of the mares who were mated with Seabiscuit throughout his brief career as a stallion. This foal, Sea Convoy, was a winner, but without a great deal of ability. He made up for his moderate racing ability by exhibiting great durability. This was a trait that was to become a trademark with foals sired by the Biscuit. Sea Convoy won only four out of 104 starts. Four of the foals in this crop raced and all of them won.

The best was the Stakes Placed filly Sea Frolic. She was first, second or third in 18 of her 25 starts. Unfortunately, there is no record of her producing a Thoroughbred foal.

The following year, 1941, was even more dismal from a racing standpoint. He had only 3 foals and only one raced. The one bright spot in this small crop was the filly Sea Anemone. Although unraced, she turned out to be a superior broodmare. She produced three Stakes Winners from six foals. All three were colts and they all became sires of Stakes Winners. Aegean and Battleground were marginal sires, but Windy Sea became a very successful sire. He had 13 Stakes Winners, including the major Stakes mare Windy's Daughter who won 13 of her 17 starts including the Hollywood Lassie, the Del Mar Debutante and the Cinderella Stakes as a two year old. At three she won two Grade 1 Stakes, The Mother Goose and the Acorn. Both races are major Stakes for three-year-old fillies.

As dismal as the racing record of his second crop of foals was, its importance paled in comparison to the big picture. December 7, 1941 ... a date that would, as President F. D. R. would vow, "live in infamy." The Japanese attack on Pearl Harbor would change the world and America would plummet headlong into World War II. Racing was suspended in California and racetracks were turned into army encampments or concentration camps. The Thoroughbred breeding industry survived, but just barely. Oblivious to the worldwide disaster, Seabiscuit continued to propagate.

The 1942 crop was finally one that the racing world had expected of the Champion. He had twenty foals, 17 of which made it to the races. Among them were four Stakes Winners and two Stakes Placed horses. That's a phenomenal 30% from foals and 35% from starters. Santa Catalina Handicap winner Sea Sovereign was one of Seabiscuit's best, but his abbreviated career of a mere eight starts was a great disappointment. He looked a great deal like his sire, especially in the head. Because of this similarity he was afforded a second career by taking the role of Seabiscuit in the 1950 movie "The Story of Seabiscuit." Also in this crop was the fine Stakes mare Sea Spray, who was also a stakes producer. Bismarck Sea, Phantom Sea and Mediterranean were also Stakes horses in that crop, but the best of the crop, and arguably the best foal of Seabiscuit was Sea Swallow, winner of four Stakes races and considered good enough to compete in the 1945 Kentucky Derby. He finished seventh out of sixteen starters and was ridden by George Wolff. Sea Swallow was out of the aforementioned fine broodmare Illeana. One of the three non-starters in the crop was the mare Sea Nymph. Half of her eight foals were of Stakes caliber.

Twelve of the thirteen foals of 1943 raced. Eight of them won and one placed. None were of any exceptional class, but two of the fillies proved to be good producers. Sea Imp had only one foal, a filly, but that filly produced four Stakes horses. Sea Maid had four foals and four winners, but the crop as a whole had to be a disappointment to Howard.

There were eighteen foals in the crop of 1944, making this Seabiscuit's second largest crop of foals. This is the crop with which the author worked at Ridgewood Ranch. There were seven winners, but only one Stakes horse in the group. That colt, Tropical Sea, showed considerable promise as a young runner. However, his career is best noted for its longevity. Perhaps he was attempting to emulate his sire as he raced until he was eleven years of age and made 142 starts, winning fifteen. A filly from the 1944 crop, Sea Song, won 19 of her 122 starts. My personal favorite, among those for which I was responsible to care for, was Sea Gold. She won two of her nine starts, but her claim to fame came as a broodmare. She had five foals and five winners, two of which won Stakes. Her best was the fine race mare Nooran, who won or placed in such major Stakes as The

Santa Marguerita, Santa Maria, Golden Poppy, etc. Numerous winners and Stakes quality horses have come from this female line right down to the present day.

In 1945 there were thirteen foals, eleven starters and ten winners. No Stakes quality hoses came from this crop, but Sea Gold's full sister Sea Treasure became the ancestress of many Stakes horses. And, as with Sea Gold, they continue to win at this time. A non-starter in the crop was the filly Sea Nun. She had five starters and five winners from six foals. One was a Stakes Winner. Again, more long lasting racers. Sea Splendor started 123 times and others raced over 50 times. Continuing the trademark of the little Biscuits.

The foals of 1946 were an undistinguished group with only four winners from eleven foals. The only moderately bright spot was My Biscuit. She did not win, but was placed in four of five starts and produced a Stakes Winner. Her colt, The Biscuit, won the Hilllsdale Handicap and fourteen of his seventy-seven starts.

In 1947 Seabiscuit had sixteen foals. Remarkably, all sixteen made it to the races. Again, Seabiscuit proved that his renowned durability was no fluke. Thirteen of them won and the other three placed. One, the fine mare Sea Garden, was a Stakes Winner. First in the Bay Meadows Lassie and The Tanforan Lassie, she was also second in the Hollywood Oaks. She is another whose descendants are still running and winning. She, too, was a daughter of the remarkable mare Illeana. Sea Novice, who won eight of her forty one starts, did better as a broodmare, producing two Stakes Winners. Probably the most remarkable accomplishment was made by the colt Bart's Rock. His name was derived from the rock under which Black Bart had hidden the handkerchief that would become his undoing. Bart's Rock placed in two minor Stakes, but the thing that distinguished him was that he raced for ten years and made an astounding 211 starts with 25 wins, 38 seconds and 39 thirds. All in all, it was a very accomplished crop.

Sadly, the 1948 crop proved to be the last for the great Seabiscuit and it was composed of only seven foals. The same number as his 1940 "Seven Little Biscuits." Six of the seven raced and five won. Sea Scholar placed in two modest Stakes, but none of the others showed much class on the track. However, again, the fine mare Illeana came to the rescue. Remember her? She produced his first foal and later his best colt in Sea Swallow and one of his best fillies in Sea Garden. Now she had a filly in Seabiscuit's final crop of foals. This was Sea Flora, winner of four races in fifty-six starts, but ending her career in cheap races at Mexico's Caliente Race Track. But, her forte proved to be as a broodmare. Bred to Hyperion's son, Orbit 11, in her first year in the breeding shed, she produced what became the most accomplished runner and the best descendant of Seabiscuit. This was Sea Orbit. He proved to be a chip off of the old block. Like his grandsire, he exhibited both extreme class and durability by winning or placing in 22 Stakes in his 67 starts. His total record, as well as his life's story, is covered in chapter 12.

The overall progeny record of the sensational racer Seabiscuit proved to be somewhat of a disappointment. There were numerous bright spots in The Biscuit's sire record and his record was considerably better than average. However, the promise he showed as a sire was never to come to fruition. From the standpoint of quality, he improved over the mares to which he was bred and he certainly added the factor of extreme soundness to his offspring. Twenty-five of his eighty-six starters raced fifty or more times. However, there were just not enough foals to earn him fame as a sire. It seemed that he would have an exciting crop of foals that would create the feeling that he was on the verge of producing a major Stakes horse. Then the next crop would be composed of runners of moderate ability.

Seabiscuit sired only 108 foals before his untimely death. This was far too few to prove his worth as a sire. Present day leading sires have that many foals in a single crop with far less success in many of the categories considered as indicative of making a successful sire. Seabiscuit proved his robust soundness by siring 80% starters from foals. This compares very favorably with 69%, the average for the breed. He sired 61% winners from foals and 77% winners from starters. The breed average is 46% and 66% respectively. As for quality, the average percentage of Stakes Placed horses from foals is 5% and from starters 7%. Seabiscuit sired 6% from foals and 13% from starters.

Howard was attempting to quickly put together a broodmare band of quality in order to help his champion become a successful sire, but the cards were stacked against his succeeding in his quest. It takes many years to develop a great band of broodmares, constantly culling and replacing its members in order to upgrade the quality. Howard simply ran out of time with the unexpected demise of Seabiscuit.

Another factor was the size of his foal crops. Most owners of champions, upon their retirement, are inundated with requests for breeding contracts. This allows them a chance to be selective and to accept only the cream of the crop. Howard owned almost every mare that produced a Seabiscuit foal. This was not a reflection of the popularity of Seabiscuit and it was not because Howard was reluctant to breed outside mares to him. It was simply a reflection of the times. There was a little disturbance, referred to as World War II, which compromised Seabiscuit's attempt at obtaining a book of mares to compliment his abilities. Ridgewood ranch is located some 600 miles north of what was then the center of the 1940's Thoroughbred breeding industry in California. The large horse vans that are so commonly used today were non-existent at that time. Horses were usually transported in small two, and often one horse trailers. Owners of the better mares were unwilling to ship 600 miles when they could breed to such proven sires as Alibhai and Beau Pere who were located close to home. Beau Pere commanded the highest priced stud fee in California at $2,500 while Alibhai and Seabiscuit were second at $1,500. An even more compelling reason for not shipping was the fact that gas was severely rationed due to the war effort. It was highly unlikely that the Ration Board would consider shipping a broodmare, to be bred, as a just cause for granting additional gas stamps.

Sadly, although The Biscuit showed great promise as a sire, he had too many obstacles to overcome. Even for the great Seabiscuit, who became famous for the many obstacles he was able to shrug off in his racing career, the quest to attain the status of a great progenitor was one victory that proved unattainable. He was far better, as a sire, than he had a right to be with all of the obstacles, but was still a disappointment to his many fans. He was, as with all great horses, expected to produce a foal in the image of his own great racing ability. He didn't do so, but neither did Man O' War, Citation, Secretariat or any of the other truly great ones. It just doesn't happen.

The Estate of Charles S. Howard held a dispersal of the Ridgewood horses on November 27, 1950. One hundred and ten hoses were cataloged, among them being twenty-one daughters of the great champion. Several proved to be bargain buys. The fine race mare Sea Spray went to L. K. Shapiro for $7,000. She produced three Stakes horses for him and was the grand-dam of several more. M. Haskell paid only $900 for Sea Nymph and she also rewarded him with three Stakes horses. Ted Tepper bid in the Stakes producer Sea Knightess for a paltry $350. However, Frank Vessels proved that he had the best eye at the sale by spending only $100 for Sea Belle. She produced the Stakes Placed winner of twelve races, Captain Bam.

Interestingly, no daughters of Illeanna, who was Ridgewood Ranch's finest producing mare, were included in the sale.

The great Kayak II had departed the scene long before the sale. He had developed into a big, powerful, impressive looking stallion. However, despite his magnificent appearance, he proved to be a major disappointment as a sire. A shy breeder, he sired very few foals and nothing that distinguished itself as a runner. In the fall of 1946 he had been sent south to Binglin Stock Farm with the hope that the milder climate may improve his fertility. It was not to be. He died of a circulatory disease before the breeding season began.

Although his daughters proved to be excellent producers and their descendants continue to be successful runners, the Seabiscuit sons are another story. Fifteen of his sons produced a paltry total of 237 foals. That's an average of less than sixteen per sire. Stakes Winner Sea Sovereign had the most foals (forty) and the largest amount of earnings ($242,649), but failed to produce a Stakes horse. Seabiscuit's best son, multiple Stakes Winner Sea Swallow, had a very unusual production record. Apparently his connections tried to emulate his sire's history of producing foals while continuing his racing career. While still racing from 1946 to 1949, he sired five foals, one each in 1947 and 1948, three in 1949 and none in 1950. He continued his stud career by siring two foals in 1951, one in 1952, none in 1953 and ended his breeding career with one 1954 foal. He had eight starters and six winners from his nine foals. They earned a total of $43,009 and one of them placed in two minor stakes races in Arizona, earning a total of $12,673 from 101 starts.

If you are looking for a bright spot in the breeding careers of the Seabiscuit sons, there isn't one. Again, his daughters came to the rescue by producing several sons who went to stud. Most of these were only marginally successful, but one proved to be the horse, that would save the bloodline and keep it going by the proverbial hair.

Sea Orbit, the most successful racing descendant of Seabiscuit, sired only 35 foals, before his untimely death. Twenty-one, of his twenty-seven starters, proved to be winners. One, Orbit Tracer, was Stakes Placed, running second in the Pomona Governor's Handicap and earning $31,388 for her five wins.

Super Orbit, a full brother to Sea Orbit, sired 52 foals with twenty-two starters and fourteen winners. Only one, Super Starlit, was a Stakes Winner. She won 14 of her 107 starts and $107,281, racing for seven years. Apparently, her long strenuous racing career compromised her ability to produce foals. From 1990 to 1996 she was bred, but "slipped" her foals every year, never producing a live foal.

Sea Fortune had nineteen foals, five starters and two winners. One non-winner, placed in a small Stakes Race in Montana.

Aegean had fifty foals. Two won minor Stakes. His half brother, Battleground, sired fifty-one foals and had one minor Stakes Winner. Both of these horses were out of Seabiscuit's daughter Sea Anemone who was unraced, but proved to be a very important producer. Her third son to enter the breeding shed was Windy Sea.

Windy Sea, owned by Harry Curland, was a successful runner, winning eight of his twelve starts and earning $47,750. He won two Stakes, The Lakes and Flowers Handicap and The Coronado Handicap, both at Hollywood Park. Unlike his grandsire, Seabiscuit, Windy Sea was afforded every opportunity to prove himself. He entered the stud in 1964 at one of the most prestigious Thoroughbred breeding farms in Southern California. That was Old English Rancho, the pride of the Johnson family. Old English has been a popular and successful breeding farm for many years and continues its operation at the present time.

"Bud" Johnson, scion of the Johnson family and current owner of Old English Rancho, describes Windy Sea as being a "medium sized chestnut horse, possessing excellent conformation and a large hip." This would explain the fact that he sired great speed and can still be found in the pedigree of racing Quarter Horses to this day. "Bud" went on to say, "Windy Sea had a very good disposition and never gave them any problems." He sounds like a typical descendant of Seabiscuit to me.

Also, unlike Seabiscuit, Windy Sea had the right numbers. He sired 291 foals over a breeding career that lasted for seventeen years. From these offspring, there were 227 starters and 163 winners. They included thirteen Stakes Winners and an additional fifteen who placed in Stakes. All told, his foals earned $3,869,426.

The brightest star in Windy Sea's resume was the great race mare Windy's Daughter. The accomplished runner won twelve of her seventeen starts; ten of which were Stakes wins. She won the Grade-1 Acorn and Mother Goose Stakes, which were two legs of the New York Racing Assn's Triple Crown. She also captured the Hollywood Lassie, the Del Mar Debutante and the Pasadena Stakes-G3, earning a total of $304,682. Undefeated in her seven starts, at two, the great filly was allotted 118 pounds on the Experimental Free Handicap and was voted Champion California-bred filly. Retired, after her equally brilliant three year-old season, she was bred to the great Secretariat in 1974. The offspring from that cross was awaited with bated breath and with great expectations. It must have been a tremendous disappointment when the filly, Centrifolia, unraced, produced only two winners from her six foals. Two of her foals were fillies and both did become Stakes producers, which was some consolation. Windy's Daughter did produce two Stakes Placed winners, from her fourteen foals, and there are dozens of high quality racers who can claim the great filly as their ancestor.

Miss Lady Bug, a year older than Windy's Daughter, was another brilliant two-year old. She finished in the money in eleven of her twelve starts at two, including eight Stakes. She captured the Nursery and Cinderella Stakes at Hollywood Park and finished second in the Del Mar Debutante, among others. Unfortunately, she produced only one live foal and he was unraced.

Numerous daughters of Windy Sea have produced Stakes quality runners. An example is Sea I'm Lucky, who was unraced, but is the dam of Stakes Winners Lucky Twist and Mixed Pleasure and the second dam of Sucha Lucky Deal and Stakes Placed Iza Beauty.

Although no descendants of Windy Sea are currently listed as standing at stud in California, Mixed Pleasure is making the bloodline available in Oregon. He was a very talented two-year old with three wins, a second and a third in seven starts. He earned $99,900 as a two year old, winning two Stakes and running second in the Hollywood Juvenile Championship Stakes-G2 He was also third in the Balboa Stakes, G3 at Del Mar. He won two races at three, running second in a Stake race. His four year-old racing season was cut short and he was retired with total earnings of $140,175. One would assume that his record, coupled with his breeding would have assured him of receiving a decent chance at stud. This was not to occur. He had two foals in 1991, both moderate winners and both fillies. Neither of them has a production record. Mixed Pleasure had one foal in each of the years of 1995, 1997, and 1999. None raced and the one filly has no production record. Chalk up another male descendant of Seabiscuit who was given little chance to continue the bloodline.

It is clear that the daughters of Seabiscuit and the female line produced by them have kept his bloodline alive. The siring record of the sons and grandsons of the Biscuit, on the other hand, can only be described as miserable. In the opinion of this author, the only exception to this statement is Windy Sea.

Sea Swallow, a son of Seabiscuit and the fine mare Illeana, won the 1944 Haggin Stakes. He is pictured with jockey Hubert S. Jones.
Photo courtesy of the Jones Family Archives

BABY BISCUIT 12

There was still snow on the ground and it was a chilly evening. We were high atop Palomar Mountain in San Diego County, California. The ranch was, to put it kindly, rustic. No electricity and no telephone. Running water, only due to gravity flow from the water tank. Of course, one had to descend down a hill, toting a can of gasoline, start the pump at the spring, fill the tank, turn off the pump and rush back up the treacherous path, praying not to freeze to death on the way up. This was not a typical Thoroughbred-breeding farm. This was an attempt to survive under pioneer conditions and to breed and raise hardy horses. Actually, this was idiotic. We survived only due to our youth, determination and good health.

The early 1960's ushered in a prosperous time for Thoroughbred racing and breeding, despite the unsettled times. What seemed to be a never-ending Vietnamese War continued. America fell in love with newly elected President John Kennedy and his beautiful wife, Jackie. The year was 1960 and two years later, Kennedy led us through the Cuban missile crises. In Dallas, Texas, it was to end much too soon; John F. Kennedy was assassinated.

But, I digress. Sea Flora was a young daughter of Seabiscuit. She was from his final crop of foals and out of the fine mare Illeanna. Illeanna had also produced his first foal and this was to be Sea Flora's first foal. The mare was showing signs of nervousness and it appeared that she was close to foaling. Armed with a kerosene lantern and a flashlight, my wife, Lillian, and I were as prepared as we could be, under the circumstances. The date was May 18, 1956.

The act of foaling was somewhat difficult as the foal had rather massive shoulders and hips, so it was necessary to give the mare assistance in the foaling process. This is fairly common with maiden mares. The foal was still lying in the ample straw bedding, wet from the amniotic fluid and had not yet bonded with his dam. I took one look at him and said to my wife: "Good lord, it's another Seabiscuit." Other than a small amount of white markings, he was the 'spitting image' of his maternal grandfather. He was immediately tagged with the stable name of "Baby Biscuit." That later was shortened to "Baby B" and, as he matured and "baby" no longer described him, he was simply called "B."

Baby B. was an energetic young colt. He stood quickly and, like his grandfather, decided that food was an important part of his young life. Sea Flora had a completely different agenda. She took one look at the little creature and decided that she had no idea what it was, but it certainly wasn't going to nurse off of her. We then milked her out to obtain the necessary colostrum and fed him with a baby bottle. After about twenty-four hours, and under restraint, she allowed him to nurse. Not the best scenario, but she eventually became a good mother to the colt who would become known as Sea Orbit.

The series of events, which resulted in the creation of this grandson of the great Seabiscuit, began two years prior to his birth. In 1954 Walter Thomson had a gelding in training at Caliente Race Track in Tijuana. His trainer, Jim Canty, advised him that the horse showed little promise and introduced him to Justine Moss. Moss was also training at Caliente and she had a mare that was at the end of her racing career. She asked if he would be interested in trading the mare for his gelding. The gelding had shown little talent so the answer was in the affirmative and the trade was made. The mare was Sea Flora, a daughter of Seabiscuit and Illeanna from the last crop of foals sired by Seabiscuit. A swap was made and Thomson had another broodmare. And what an addition to his band of mares she became. As fate would have it, the gelding raced successfully shortly after the trade, but that's what generally seems to happen in this business. Justine Moss was best known for her ownership of the great California-bred Kentucky Derby winner Morvich. She was a personal friend of the well-known Kentucky breeder Elizabeth Daingerfield at whose farm Morvich stood. In 1939 Miss Daingerfield asked Justine if she would like to have the aging Morvich as a sire on her California breeding farm. According to Kaye Erickson's article in the February, 1946 issue of The Thoroughbred of California, "Miss Mosse accepted the offer and brought Morvich to California in a trailer behind her passenger car. The intrepid horsewoman made the trip alone. During the journey she was plagued with ice and snow. So severe was the weather that one day she was able to travel only forty miles."

Sea Flora was shipped to Mr. Thomson's Rancho Felicia in Santa Inez, California. Thomson had recently acquired Orbit 11, a direct son of the great English progenitor Hyperion. Sea Flora was to be bred to that promising young stallion.

A little background on this remarkable man, Walter J. Thomson, and then back to the Sea Orbit story. Born in Johannesburg, South Africa on April 30, 1911, Walter James Thomson followed in his father's footsteps by becoming an importer. With the divorce of his parents, his mother brought four year-old Walter back to her home in America. He first came to California in 1915 and at the age of sixteen went to Hamburg, Germany in order to serve an apprenticeship in the importing business. He worked for a Los Angeles importer for a couple of years and then began his own very successful importing business.

Walter's first experience into Thoroughbred breeding was is 1942 when he attended an auction at Santa Anita Racetrack. He purchased a six year-old mare named Ebony Eyes for $135.00. She was a winner, sired by a Kentucky Derby winner and in foal to the stallion Grog. The foal she was carrying, Sandalwood, became Walter's first winner. Grog was sired by Seabiscuit's sire, Hard Tack. Additionally Broomstick was close up in their respective pedigrees. No wonder Tom Smith presented Grog to reporters and claimed him to be Seabiscuit. They were similar in conformation and Grog saved Seabiscuit from becoming stressed by the constant stream of onlookers.

In 1941 Walter had an estate close enough to Santa Anita that he could hear the races being called from his home. He began his venture by keeping his horses on the estate. By 1946 it became obvious that he needed more property to house his ever-increasing band of horses. At that time he purchased 320 acres in the beautiful Santa Ynez Valley, just a short distance from the quaint Danish town of Solvang. He named the breeding farm Rancho Felicia and it is now the oldest operating Thoroughbred breeding farm in that area.

In 1991 his beloved wife Holly passed away. They had been married for fifty-four years. Walter was devastated. I would call him and hear a dull, listless voice with no sign of his former enthusiasm and love of life. He was depressed and I was concerned for his well-being. Then one day I called him and he sounded like his old self. I asked him what had occurred to effect the change. He said, "I just met the most wonderful lady." That lady, Mary Jean, was to become Walter's second wife in 1994. What a near miraculous effect she had upon Walter. I doubt that he would have reached his current age of ninety-five without the TLC Mary Jean has administered. Of course Walter, with his quick wit, says, "I'm only ninety-five."

Meanwhile, back on the ranch, I was sitting by the wood stove. This was the only heat available. I was reading the February, 1955 issue of "The Thoroughbred of California" by the light from a kerosene lantern. In the classified ads, under the heading of "Thoroughbreds For Lease" I saw an ad that read as follow:

STALLION AND MARES FOR LEASE.
Breeder planning extended stay abroad will consider leasing fashionably-bred stallion of the highest class, together with ten excellent mares, share basis, to financially responsible breeder having adequate facilities. Write Box 266. The Thoroughbred of Calif.

I took one look at that ad. And it just seemed to be talking to me. Well. Actually, it took more than one look. We were running out of kerosene. I rushed into the bedroom, awoke my wife and read the good news to her. "Are you crazy?" she said. "Read what it says. Financially responsible? Adequate facilities? How on earth do you think that refers to us?" I don't know, I replied. "I just know that this is our destiny and we are meant to have these horses." I answered the ad, requesting information on the pedigrees of the individuals and, when Mr. Thomson responded, and I saw the name Sea Flora by Seabiscuit, I knew that it was meant to be.

Well, things moved rather rapidly and the next thing I knew, Walter, along with his lovely wife, Holly, were planning a trip to Palomar Mountain to meet the "financially responsible" couple with the "adequate facilities." Woops! Now what do we do? At that point, even I felt that it was a hopeless situation. Our finances were nil. The facility? Well, there was a thousand acres of land with no horse fencing and no stabling. The house had no electricity and we were hosting guests who would be deciding our future. My wife made coffee on the wood stove, poured it into an electric coffee pot, that hadn't experienced electricity for over a year, and served it to our guests. Hopefully, they would think we were at least close to being civilized. Actually, I doubt that we fooled them at all, but we took an immediate liking to one another. They decided, excepting for the coffee, that we had integrity and could be trusted with their livestock. Walter and I finalized the lease while Holly enjoyed swinging in a tire attached to a large tree in front of the house. What a delightful couple.

In writing about Walter Thomson, it occurred to me that as you travel through life you might witness greatness without being aware of it. I consider myself fortunate in witnessing and being aware of the greatness in this remarkable man.

Now back to the Sea Orbit story. Sea Flora, once she determined that this motherhood thing was normal and that this strange little creature meant her no harm, became a good mother. The colt developed into a handsome individual and, in the fall of his first year moved with us to Rancho Felicia. The following summer he continued his trip north, when we moved to Sacramento. He had been inspected, and accepted for the prestigious California Thoroughbred Breeders Association select yearling sale at Del Mar, California. It wasn't to be. Shortly before the sale he suffered a cosmetic injury, which necessitated his being withdrawn from the sale. What to do?

Here was a handsome colt, which I was certain had the Seabiscuit heart and he had a knot on his cannon bone.

Sea Orbit was entered, as a two year-old, in the January Mixed Sale at Pomona, California. I had a veterinary certificate, stating that the bump on the shin was simply a calcification involving no tendons or ligaments and was cosmetic. It didn't help. Leading owners and trainers came to look at him. Rex Ellsworth, breeder and owner of the great Swaps, inspected him. He shook his head and said, "What a shame." The prospective buyers took one look at the bump and stayed away in droves. He sold for a paltry $2,500. My heart sank. Then I discovered that a friend of ours, Willis Merrill of Wonder Y Ranch, had purchased him. I had no idea that he was planning on buying anything at the sale when I said to him, "Willis, if I have ever seen a Stakes colt, this is it." He took me at my word and bid him in.

He was turned over to trainer John Leavitt, and his career was to begin. Unfortunately, Leavitt's impression of the colt was not a positive one. Much like Fitzimmons attitude toward Seabiscuit, Leavitt felt that Sea Orbit lacked any serious talent.

Sea Orbit had many minor problems as a two-year old. He shin-bucked several times and had a shin splint. We arranged to have him shipped to the veterinary college at the University of California at Davis, California. They removed the splint problem and he returned to training. The delays kept him from racing as a two-year old and he made his first start on January 16, 1959 at Santa Anita, where his grandsire had made his final start. He ran second in a maiden five thousand dollar claiming event. His odds were $25.30 to one. Well, at least it was a beginning and he was eight lengths ahead of the third horse in the twelve-horse field. After two more undistinguished starts, he headed north to Tanforan racetrack on the San Francisco peninsula. His fourth start was a winning one. He won by two and one half lengths over a modest field of $5,000 claimers. Nine days later he tackled a slightly better class of horses in a winner's race for a $7,000 claiming tag. Again, he won. This time he was the favorite and won by half a length. Three weeks later he again jumped up in class and attempted an allowance race. He was second, but his race time was improving dramatically with each successive start.

Sea Orbit next shipped south to Hollywood Park, where he won two races, including an allowance at a mile. He finished his three year-old racing career with four wins, three seconds and three thirds in sixteen starts. It was time for some rest and relaxation. He was given a short vacation and began his four-year old season on January 7 at Santa Anita. Seven starts at that track resulted in a pair of nice allowance wins. In one he defeated Ellsworth's Like Magic, a full brother to Swaps. One can only wonder if Ellsworth regretted dismissing Sea Orbit at the sale, or for that matter, if he even remembered the incident.

Again, the grandson of the legend headed north. This time Bay Meadows was his destination and he had finally climbed the class ladder and made his presence felt in Stakes races. April 16, 1960 was a red-letter day for Sea Orbit. He won the mile and a sixteenth Governor's Handicap. Overlooked by the public, he paid $36.40 for a two-dollar wager. He showed that his win was no fluke by running a close second in his next start, also a Stakes race. Picking up weight he then won the William P. Kyne Memorial Handicap. The chart reads: "Sea Orbit, well in hand for the first half mile while being rated back of the leaders, was taken to the outside for racing room on the far turn and under vigorous handling, steadily wore down the pacemakers to take command a furlong out, responding gamely to mild urging, increased his advantage with every stride." Setting a new track record of 1:47 for the mile and one eighth, the little bay colt was giving notice that he was carrying the Seabiscuit banner into a new generation of runners. Coincidentally, His track record was set on May 16, 1960. On April 16, 1938, Seabiscuit had set the track record of 1:49 for 1 1/8 miles at Bay Meadows.

Once again heading south to Hollywood Park, Sea Orbit immediately won another Stake and then ran a close second in the prestigious Inglewood Handicap. He came out of that race with an injury that ended his four-year old career. His record: Five wins, four seconds and a third in thirteen starts, defeating Fleet Nasrullah, Prize Host, First Balcony and a host of other talented runners.

After a six-month recuperative period, he was ready to renew his career at Santa Anita, making his first start on January 2. It took a couple of races for him to regain his winning form and after two wins at Santa Anita he was entered in the March 25, 1961 San Francisco Mile at Golden Gate Fields. Four and Twenty, ridden by the great jockey Johnny Longden, was favored at forty cents on the dollar. He was a winter-book favorite for the Kentucky Derby and undefeated at that time. Sea Orbit was the second choice of the fans, but nobody told him that. Carrying top weight, he sat just behind the fast pace of undefeated Four and Twenty. Into the stretch the favorite was in the lead and looked to be a sure winner. They hadn't counted on Sea Orbit's explosive burst of speed. Within strides he was four in front and drawing away. A startled Four and Twenty, having never experienced a horse who could accelerate and pass him finished fifth, eighteen lengths back and he was withdrawn from Derby consideration.

Sea Orbit continued racing in Stakes races, winning the Inglewood Handicap and placing in several others, but by August it was again time for some rest. He had won five races that season, set a new track record and defeated major stars T.

V. Lark, Four and Twenty, First Balcony, Dress Up and New Policy, among others.

In January of 1962 he renewed his racing career as a six year old. It was again at Santa Anita. This time it took several starts for him to regain his best form and he didn't win until May at Hollywood Park where he won an allowance race. He followed that up by running second to Ellsworth's Prove It, in the Inglewood Handicap. Windy Sands, T. V. Lark, Crazy Kid and Olden Times trailed him home.

Del Mar was his next stop and he was spectacular. Although his best races had been at middle distances (a mile to a mile and an eighth) he was entered in the six furlong Bing Crosby Handicap. The Bing Crosby is one of the most sought after prizes for sprinters and was named for the famed movie star who was a co-founder of Del Mar Racetrack. Sea Orbit was required to pack top weight, giving up to eight pounds to the others. Ray York, who had become his regular and most successful rider, rode him. Sea Orbit ran in fifth position until deep in the stretch. With a burst of speed he charged past the leaders, winning by half a length. The time was an astounding 1:08 4/5. Up until that time, August 18, it was the fastest time in the United States for that distance in 1962. Unfortunately for Sea Orbit, that record was short lived as Crazy Kid set a new world record in the next race.

Fifteen days later, in the Del Mar Handicap, he was asked to carry high weight of 122 pounds, giving from two to twelve pounds to the other six horses. Crazy Kid was assigned a two-pound break in the weights from Sea Orbit, despite coming off of a world record performance. He defeated Sea Orbit by three-fourths of a length.

By October he was again in Northern California at Golden Gate Fields. He carried top weight of 123 pounds in the one mile William G. Gilmore Handicap and galloped home, by an increasing three lengths in 1:34 4/5. In his next race, The Golden Gate Handicap, he was assigned 126 pounds, giving from ten to sixteen pounds to the rest of the horses. It was too much to ask of him. He finished second to Mandate who carried only 114 pounds.

Moving across the San Francisco Bay to Bay Meadows, he carried 124 pounds to victory in the San Carlos Handicap. Coming right back in The Children's Hospital Handicap, he carried 126 pounds to a two length romp. One week later he was assigned 129 pounds for the top race of the meeting, The Bay Meadows Handicap. He gave from twelve to twenty-six pounds to the remainder of the field and it was run in deep mud. No problem. The Racing Form chart reads, "Sea Orbit, had speed, took the lead when ready, drew clear and saving ground, drew out in the stretch to win easily." It was 3 ½ lengths back to the second horse, carrying seventeen pounds less than the champ. His record for the year was six wins, four seconds and a third in eighteen starts. The list of stars he had defeated was growing in length and included Prove It (twice), T. V. Lark, Windy Sands and Olden Times.

As he had each year, he began his final year of racing at Santa Anita. He was now seven years of age. It was at the same age, and at the same track that Seabiscuit concluded his brilliant career. His first start of 1963 was an ambitious one. He ran sixth to such stars as Crozier, Olden Times and Native Diver, but did defeat Kentucky Derby winner Tomy Lee. Ten days later he won the National Date Festival Handicap, defeating another Kentucky Derby victor in Decidedly. A week later he was to make the sixty-seventh, and final start of his lengthy career. It was in the Santa Catalina Handicap. Prior to the race, his owner, Willis Merrill announced that "Win, lose or draw, this will be Sea Orbit's final start." Win it he did, carrying 123 pounds to a half-length victory. Favorite Olden Times finished seventh of the eight runners. The fans gave him a standing ovation, as they had his grandfather, at the same track and at the same age, twenty-three years earlier. He came out of his last start in great shape and was one of the favorites for the soon to be run Santa Anita Handicap, having defeated most of the runners pointing for that great race. It is a shame that he wasn't given the opportunity to attempt to emulate his grandfather by retiring after a win in that race.

Sea Orbit concluded his racing career with a record of 67 starts with 22 wins, 13 seconds and 7 thirds. He won or placed in twenty-two Stakes Races. Twelve of these races are now identified as being Grade 1, 2 or 3. At the time he was running, races were not Graded. His earnings of $291,275 appear miniscule by today's purses. However, purses were considerably smaller at that time. For instance, when he won The Bing Crosby Stakes, which had attracted the best sprinters in the country, it was worth $12,500. By 2004 it was a Grade-1 race worth $244,000. The Del Mar Handicap, now a Grade-2 race worth $250,000 was run for $30,000 at the time Sea Orbit ran in it. In researching the purse money in the early 1960's as compared with 2004, I discovered that the average purse of the races won by Sea Orbit is now 7.18 times greater in value. By today's standards, Sea Orbit's earnings would total $2,091,355. Not too shabby for a $2,500 bargain colt. I was recently informed of an additional honor of which I had been unaware. Pam Merrill Cookson, granddaughter of Sea Orbit's owners, Willis and Peg Merrill informed me that the city of Del Mar, California named a street "Sea Orbit Lane."

Like Seabiscuit, Sea Orbit did it all. His career spanned many years and a great number of races. He met the best of his era and defeated most of them. He won about a third of his races and was in the money in two-thirds. He carried high weights and was a favorite of the fans. He deserved the opportunity to retire to the breeding farm and be given the opportunity to assure that Seabiscuit's bloodlines would live on.

It wasn't to be. But, who knew it at that time. His first crop of foals arrived in 1964. There were six of them, one less that in Seabiscuit's first crop of foals. The quality of the mares to which he was bred was, to put it kindly, modest. Three of his foals raced and two won. His 1965 crop was his largest. Nine of the ten foals raced and six won. One, Orbit Tracer, placed in the Governor's Cup Handicap at Pomona. The 1966 crop dropped to five foals. Four raced and they all won, but none had a great deal of ability. Seven of the eight foals in the 1967 crop raced. Five won. He had only two foals in 1968. One raced and won fourteen of her sixty-five starts. There were two winners from three foals in 1969.

Sea Orbit's final crop was comprised of one filly, which won four of her eighteen starts. Tragically, Sea Orbit died in 1969. In perfect health and only thirteen years of age, he had a reaction from a vaccine, collapsed to the ground and shattered his shoulder. Like his grandfather Seabiscuit before him, he died young leaving too few foals to assure the survival of his bloodlines. Thirty-five foals in seven crops were too few to jump-start his career as a stallion.

About the best thing one can say about Sea Orbit's stud career is that he produced sound horses (77% percent starters from foals), which had the will to win (78% winners from starters).

Ten of his fifteen daughters produced foals. Miss Marquis a daughter of the Nearco mare *Ndara, produced a colt reminiscent of the Seabiscuit ilk. He made 115 starts, winning a dozen and earning over $65,000. Another of her sons raced seventy-eight times. Her line however has died out. Another whose line appears to have come to an end is Miss Sea Orbit, although she has a granddaughter, Delphi Dolly, who has five daughters still young enough to produce foals. Bit O' Dell is another whose line is hanging on by a thread. The same applies to Sea Bonnet, another daughter of *Ndara.

Interestingly, the three Sea Orbit daughters who still have a slim chance of continuing the bloodlines were all produced from mares bred to him and owned by Walter Thomson, co-breeder of Sea Orbit. All of the other daughters of Sea Orbit appear to have met dead-ends as far as their production records are concerned.

On January 17, 2006 a Merrill/Sea Orbit exhibit opened at the Valley Center Historical Museum in Valley Center, California. It was scheduled as a six-month display of memorabilia dealing with Sea Orbit and Wonder Y Ranch, which was the name of the Merrill Thoroughbred Breeding Farm located in Valley Center.

SEA ORBIT
(Seabiscuits' best decendant)
(Bred by Walter J. Thomson and William H. Nichols)

		=Hyperion (Gb) 30
	*Orbit 2nd	
	(1945)	=Olifa (Gb) 30
Sea Orbit, B, C		
Foaled May 18, 1956		Seabiscuit 33
In California	Sea Flora	
	(1948)	Illeanna 32

Race Record

Race Record in North America

1959	16	4	3	3	$14,475
1960	13	5	4	1	$78,800
1961	17	5	2	2	$96,800
1962	18	6	4	1	$78,050
1963	3	2	0	0	$23,150
Totals	67	22	13	7	$291,275 (SSI=14.91)

1961	1st	Inglewood H ($50,000)
1960	1st	William P. Kyne Memorial H *Nt ($40,000)
1963	1st	Santa Catalina H ($25,000)
1960	1st	Golden State Breeders' H ($20,000)
1960	1st	Governor's H ($20,000, Bm)
1961	1st	Golden State Breeders' H ($20,000)
1962	1st	Bay Meadows H ($20,000)
1962	1st	Children's Hospital H ($15,000)
1962	1st	William G. Gilmore H ($15,000)
1962	1st	Bing Crosby H (1 Div) ($12,500)
1961	1st	San Francisco Mile H ($10,000)
1962	1st	San Carlos H ($10,000, Bm)
1960	2nd	Inglewood H ($50,000)
1962	2nd	Inglewood H ($50,000)
1962	2nd	Del Mar H ($30,000)
1960	2nd	Bay Meadows H ($20,000)
1962	2nd	Golden Gate H ($20,000)
1961	2nd	Albany H ($15,000)
1961	2nd	William Molter Memorial H ($15,000)
1961	3rd	Californian S ($100,000)
1961	3rd	American H ($50,000)
1962	3rd	Golden State Breeders' H ($20,000)
1960		Ntr Bay Meadows 9.00f 1 47 0

Sea Orbit was the best descendant of Seabiscuit.

Photo courtesy of The California Thoroughbred magazine

A street in Del Mar, California was named for the outstanding grandson of Seabiscuit.

Photo courtesy of The Merrill Family

ON TO HOLLYWOOD

*G*reat care was taken by the author to assure that her book, "Seabiscuit: An American Legend" would be properly depicted on the silver screen. She selected Universal Studios from a number of choices. Gary Ross was selected to direct and also to write the screenplay. Hillenbrand served as a consultant on the screenplay and provided research material.

The selection of the actors to represent the principle characters was brilliantly accomplished. Jeff Bridges was to play Charles Howard. In order to accurately portray the part, he discussed it with Laura Hillenbrand and even carried Howard's wallet in his pocket, to get a feel of the man. Laura had been given the wallet by the Howard family and loaned it to Bridges. While Bridges did an admirable acting job, the Howard he portrayed was much more flamboyant than the Howard I knew. His great-grandson, Kittridge Collins was in agreement. In a San Francisco Chronicle article he said, "He was really kind of a stoic guy. I guess they wanted him to be glib and sexy and that type of thing. Chris Cooper would have made the perfect Howard if he weren't already cast as Smith. They couldn't have two quiet guys because there wouldn't be any lines in the movie." Toby Maguire "became" Red Pollard by immersing himself in the daily life of a jockey, learning the riding style and losing enough weight to look the part, although he was already trim in build from his athletic Spiderman role. Chris Cooper did an excellent job portraying "Silent" Tom Smith. Leading jockey Gary Stevens proved to all that he had here-to-for hidden talents beyond those displayed in his regular profession. His portrayal of George Woolf was outstanding. Jockey Chris McCarron acted as a consultant for the racing scenes and played the part of War Admiral's rider, Charley Kurtsinger, in the match race scenes. I felt that Elizabeth Banks received far too little credit for her role as Marcela Howard. She portrayed her so beautifully that it could have been Marcela recreating her life from over a half a century ago. William Macy added humor to the film, with his zany portrayal of the radio personality Tick Tock McGoughlin. Oddly enough, Macy was the movie's only actor nominated for an Academy Award and his was the only character that was fictionalized. Several different horses, which were selected because of their similarity to the Biscuit, portrayed Seabiscuit.

The movie was filmed in numerous locations. Several were in southern California, including Hemet, Valley Springs and the racetracks Santa Anita and Fairplex. Fairplex was used to film the stable scenes. Saratoga Springs in New York and Keeneland Race Course in Lexington, Kentucky were also filming locations. Keeneland was transformed into Pimlico, the site of the great match race with War Admiral. Katherine Kennedy, co-producer with Frank Marshall, said that they chose Keeneland because of its "timelessness." "We wanted a race track that had not been too modernized," Kennedy stated. "Keeneland offered us that opportunity." A Keeneland Press

Release of November 13, 2002 related the following interesting story about the filming.

"The crew applied some real ingenuity for re-creating the crowded grandstand for the match race in Keeneland's 7000 seat venue."

"Typically, movies use two-dimensional cardboard cutouts to replicate crowd scenes," says Joe Biggens, chief technician for the grandstand scene. "However, that wouldn't work here because of the way the camera swings around the turns of the racetrack. If we did that, the audience was going to see the crowd in two-dimensions. So we needed to come up with a way to create a crowd that could be easily shipped and set up.

The solution was inflatable mannequins and it is the first time this technique has been employed in the movies. Biggens and his crew dressed each mannequin in long-sleeved T-shirts with khaki or blue suits silk-screened on them. An artist in Simi Valley, California, painted the masks that served as the dummy's faces and each was topped off with a hat."

The film followed the book as much as possible, considering the time restrictions imposed by the media. If all of the memorable parts of the Hillenbrand book had been included in the movie, it would have been several hours longer than its length of 134 minutes. The racing scenes were spectacular and true to life, thanks in great part to Chris McCarron's consultation and to Gary Ross's insistence that the races be portrayed exactly as they had been run. Through ingenious camera work, Ross puts the audience right into the race. The movie was arguably the best racing movie ever.

Having said that, I must admit that there were several parts of the movie with which I disagreed. I thought that one of the finest lines, in the book, was sadly omitted. As Pollard limped up to the crippled Seabiscuit, upon his return to Ridgewood Ranch, he said, "Well Pops, we have four good legs between us." How much extra time would it have taken to include that in the picture? Another error was in describing War Admiral as being eighteen hands tall and Seabiscuit as fifteen hands. Any horseman knows that an eighteen hand Thoroughbred would be a candidate for the Guinness Book of Records. In actuality, War Admiral was measured at exactly 15 hands 2–1/4 inches at the time of his Triple Crown win. At the most he may have grown another inch during the seventeen months before the Pimlico match race. Seabiscuit was measured at 15 hands 2 inches. That's not a great deal of difference in height and a far cry from the twelve inches stated in the movie.

There were several other errors in the movie, which should have been caught by the advisors. One was when Seabiscuit was put on a "hot walker." In 1936 hot walkers were two-legged humans, not the current four-armed machines. Others were the use of twine on the bales of bedding straw and goggles on the jockeys. Twine did not replace baling wire until many years later and the jockeys did not wear goggles at that time. I can forgive the inclusion of the goggles, because of the safety factor, but not the other errors. It also made it appear that the ill-fated young Frankie was Howard's only child, which is untrue. Probably my biggest objection was the depicting of Seabiscuit as a vicious, wild-eyed rogue at the time that Howard and Smith came into his life. There were a few other things in the movie that were not true to life, but that's Hollywood, I guess. However, it faithfully followed the book and the lives of the principle characters much more closely than most movies do and still gets my vote as the finest horseracing movie I've seen.

When discussing the book and the movie with Red's nephew, John C. Pollard, I asked him if there was anything in them that disturbed the Pollard family or with which they disagreed. His response was a strong affirmative. They felt that

Red did not fail as a boxer, as it was claimed that he did. As mentioned in the chapter dealing with Red, his daughter has a box full of boxing medals that he earned. Also, they felt that Red was not portrayed as he really was. He was not a quiet, angry man. He was a comic with a great sense of Irish humor and was quick on his responses. Another bone of contention was when Red's father turns to his wife and calls her Agnes. That was the name of Red's wife. His mother was Edith. Also, it was not Marcela Howard who placed the crucifix around Red's neck just prior to the Santa Anita Handicap. It was Pollard's wife, Agnes. However, the most disturbing thing, to Red's family, was that the movie portrayed them as abandoning him when he was sixteen. John says that this is not true. He ran away to become a jockey.

In 1950, Seabiscuit was featured in another movie. Titled "The Story of Seabiscuit," it starred Shirley Temple as the fictionalized daughter of Seabiscuit's trainer. Actor Barry Fitzgerald portrayed the trainer. Fitzgerald is the charming Irish actor who played the priest, opposite Bing Crosby, in Going My Way. Visualizing Fitzgerald as "Silent" Tom Smith takes imagination. "Silent" is not even close to describing the way the actor portrayed Smith. Lon McAllister played the Pollard role. The picture was really a fictionalized love story using the Seabiscuit popularity to draw viewers. Alas, even Seabiscuit and the ever-popular Shirley Temple could not convince viewers of its authenticity. The one bright spot was the use of the actual Seabiscuit race footage in the film. The film was in color, but the race footage was black and white, so the viewers knew when they were actually seeing Seabiscuit. For the non-racing scenes, Sea Sovereign, a son of the champion, portrayed his sire.

But, returning to the more recent movie, the promotional material was well done and prolific. The premiere opened with great anticipation. Actually, there were three premieres, plus the special White House showing. On Saturday, July 19, 2003 there was a "Home Town Premiere" in Willits, California. It was a daring decision to risk showing the movie to what could be a critical crowd. Nearby Ridgewood Ranch and Seabiscuit had put Willits on the map in the 1940's. Many in the audience had personal connections with the principle characters and those who didn't certainly knew someone who had lived the story. The day began with a walking tour of Ridgewood Ranch. Then it was on to the small, local theatre. There was a red carpet on the sidewalk, leading to the entrance. The theatre was packed and celebrities were introduced, including members of the Howard family. Finally, the movie began. It's the only movie I've attended where the audience cried, smiled and actually cheered. It was a hit with this most critical audience.

The following day the film was premiered in Saratoga Springs, New York and Lexington, Kentucky. It received a great reception and positive reviews in both areas.

Probably the most significant effect that the movie had was the sensitive depiction of the people during the great depression. Many men suffered from an inferiority complex. They were unable to provide for their families and felt a sense of emasculation. This feeling is evident in many scenes, especially those dealing with Pollard. The sense of pride and the unwillingness to ask for help was a typical trait of the era and was well portrayed by the actors playing the parts of Smith and Pollard.

Seabiscuit, the motion picture, garnered seven Academy Award nominations. In addition to Best Picture, the popular film was nominated for art direction, cinematography, costume design, film editing, sound and adapted screenplay.

In December the picture was released in DVD. Within four weeks the "Seabiscuit" DVD became the top selling live-action drama on the market, generating $15 million more in sales than it did at the box office.

Steven Spielberg, Laura Hillenbrand and Toby Maguire were invited to attend a special premier of the Seabiscuit movie, as well as dinner at The White House as guests of President George and Laura Bush.

Photo courtesy of Laura Hillenbrand

THE 14 ARTISTS

The charismatic Seabiscuit has been the subject of numerous talented equine artists. In the opinion of this writer, there have been mixed results.

R. H. PALENSKE was one of the earlier artists who depicted "The Biscuit." Palenske was a newspaper illustrator for over twenty years when, as the story goes, he came upon a piece of scrap copper. He began scratching a picture on it with one of his wife's sewing needles. He was fascinated with the results and diligently worked, over a lengthy period of time, to perfect his technique. The process is known as drypoint etching.

Palenske gained world fame with his art and, only four years after his first experiment with the method, was invited to stage a one-man show at The Smithsonian Institute. The Library of Congress has also placed five of his prints in preservation for posterity.

An avid outdoorsman, he is best known for his beautiful etchings depicting wild animals and majestic landscapes. He also completed works of many domestic animals, including several famous Thoroughbreds. Man O' War and Seabiscuit were both subjects of his artistic talent. Unfortunately, in my opinion, his depiction of Seabiscuit did not do the champion justice. Seabiscuit had a head of great beauty. His forehead was wide between his large expressive eyes and he was blessed with a classic profile. Palenske had a tendency to draw horse's heads with a slight filling below the eyes, giving the subject a rather common head. His Seabiscuit etchings were no exception.

C. W. ANDERSON is a noted artist and author who has done excellent work over a period of several years. He is best noted as the Author of the "Billy and Blaze" series of children's books. He also wrote "Bay, Black and Chestnut." This book, published in 1939, profiles many great horses, including Man O' War. In 1940 Anderson wrote "Deep Through the Heart." This book profiled "twenty valiant horses" with lithographs of each. Seabiscuit was one of his selections. He titled the chapter "Seabiscuit and Red, A double comeback."

FRED STONE has been successfully painting Thoroughbred horses since 1976. Both The Los Angeles Daily News and The Chicago Tribune have called him the most successful painter of horses in the world. It has been said that more people own a Fred Stone print than any other artist in history. More than eighty thousand of his limited edition prints have been sold and he is still going strong. He recently completed a Seabiscuit collage, which is offered as a limited edition print or as a limited edition canvas lithograph. While the painting is very attractive, I was surprised at its lack of accuracy. The painting includes the famous stretch run of the Seabiscuit/War Admiral match race. War Admiral was a very dark brown, nearly black, horse. Stone has him pictured as a light bay. He has also taken the liberty of shortening the stirrups on the two horses to the length used at the current time. Jockeys rode with longer stirrups than they do today. Also, they did not wear goggles at that time. Despite its lack of accuracy, it is a very attractive and popular print and Seabiscuit does look like Seabiscuit.

RICHARD STONE REEVES was born in New York City in 1919 and has probably been commissioned to paint more famous Thoroughbreds than any other artist in history. His big break, as an equine artist, was being commissioned to paint the 1947 Horse of the Year, Armed. The portrait was prominently displayed in Life Magazine and Reeves fame was assured.

When President Ronald Reagan and Nancy Reagan made a state visit to Windsor Castle in 1982, they presented H. M. Queen Elizabeth 11 with a gift of a Richard Stone Reeves original. Reeves depicts his horses with accuracy. Virtually all of the horses he paints are perfectly posed in a profile view as in a professional photograph. The background is usually an idyllic pastoral setting and his painting of Seabiscuit follows this pattern. He also painted Man O' War and War Admiral in this manner. Owners and breeders of many of the worlds greatest Thoroughbreds have had Reeves paint their prized runners. They are among the most discerning of patrons and the fact that they continue to commission him is proof of his ability to artistically depict his subjects. (Author's Note: Sadly, after this was written, Richard Stone Reeves passed away on October 7, 2005 at the age of eighty-five.)

CHRISTINE PICAVET was genetically destined to become an equine artist. She was the product of an artistic family and was born in Paris, France. She showed a love for horses at a young age and became a show rider and a riding instructor. She grew up in Villard de Lans, a ski resort in the Alps and eventually moved to Chantilly, which is a major Thoroughbred center in France. Here she worked as an exercise rider for top French stables and continued painting horses. Christine continued riding and painting when she moved to New York and eventually to California. There she worked for Hall of Fame trainer

Charles Whittingham. She married an equine veterinarian and finally retired from her riding chores. It was just before the birth of their son, Eric that she began painting horses as a full time profession. Her knowledge of horses has proven to be a great advantage to her in properly depicting her subjects. Her Seabiscuit painting shows him crossing the finish line in his final start.

FRANKLIN BROOKE VOSS was born in 1880. A contemporary of the great English sporting painter Alfred Munnings, Voss was considered to have been one of the finest American equine artists. He studied art at the Art Student's League in New York. He had the good fortune to be born into a wealthy family of horsemen and became an excellent rider himself. From an early age he foxhunted and rode in both flat and steeplechase races. His family connections included many of the most prominent names in Thoroughbred racing, including the Whitneys and the Vanderbilts. He was commissioned to paint many famous racehorses, including Seabiscuit and his grandsire, Man O' War. The Voss painting of Seabiscuit, with Red Pollard in the saddle, is an especially fine likeness of the horse and of the jockey. It is featured in the book "Seabiscuit, the saga of a great champion." This book, authored by B. K. Beckwith, with drawings by Howard Brodie was published in 1940, the year Seabiscuit retired from racing. Voss rode to the hounds his entire life, literally. He died of a heart attack, at the age of seventy-two, doing what he enjoyed most, riding in a foxhunt.

HUGHLETTE "TEX" WHEELER was born in Florida in 1900. As a young man his work as a ranch-hand generated his interest in western art subjects. He studied in Chicago and his talent for sculpture won him a scholarship to study in Paris, France. When he returned to his native country he settled in Cleveland, Ohio, where he opened a studio. Eventually he moved west, first to the Rincon Ranch in Arizona and then on to Los Angeles.

Wheeler became renowned as a sculptor who specialized in western themes and horses in particular. Many of his best-known works depicted cowboys busting broncos. His sculpture of Will Rogers, in cowboy gear, is one of his greatest and most popular works. However, his most famous sculpture is the renowned life-size statue of Seabiscuit, which was commissioned by Charles S. Howard in 1939. The finished product was an amazingly accurate depiction of the great champion. Two copies were cast in bronze. One is at Santa Anita Park in California. Appropriately, alongside Seabiscuit stands Wheelers' statue of famed jockey George Wolff who rode the champion in the famous match race with War Admiral. The second copy was erected next to Seabiscuit's stallion barn at Ridgewood Ranch. It was eventually donated to The National Museum for racing at Saratoga, New York.

"Tex" Wheeler returned to his native state of Florida, where he died in 1955 at the age of fifty-five.

JO-ELLEN is a multi-talented artist from Maryland, home of the Preakness. Reportedly, she first showed artistic talent at the tender age of eighteen months. She had many interests during her youthful years, some of which were diverse in character. She studied ballet and the violin. She excelled at archery and enjoyed shooting. Photography was an interest and she seriously considered becoming an archaeologist. However, despite all of the various and diverse interests, her passion and concentration on art never wavered. Jo-Ellen is a very talented artist. However, if you are looking for a conformation painting of Seabiscuit, you need to look farther. Her rendition is stylistic and it appears, to this writer, that Seabiscuit is galloping on a cobblestone track.

HOWARD BRODIE. What a visual rush the name Howard

Brodie triggers. Brodie was born in Oakland, California in 1915 and attended the California School of Fine Arts. My first memories of Brodie were of his sketches in the sports section of a San Francisco newspaper. It was about that time that my grandfather became acquainted with him in a San Bruno bar near the old Tanforan racetrack. When Brodie learned that his acquaintance had a grandson who was a racing fan, he quickly rendered a pencil sketch of four horses straining at the finish line. The framed drawing hangs in my home as a prized possession.

Brodie was well known as a sports artist in the San Francisco bay area, but he was soon to become internationally famous for his depiction of American soldiers during World War II. At age twenty-seven he enlisted in the army and was assigned to sketch war scenes for the new army magazine, "Yank." He continued to sketch service men in Korea and Vietnam and his sketches are in The Library of Congress and The New Britain Museum of American Art. In 2001 he was elected to the Hall of Fame Laureates of The Society of Illustrators. His Seabiscuit connection was as the illustrator for the popular book "Seabiscuit: The Saga of a Great Champion" by B. K. Beckwith. Seventeen of his sketches adorn the pages of this fine book.

THOMAS ALLEN PAULY is a Chicago born artist who has been prolific in portraying all segments of the racing world. Pauly studied with numerous equine artists and attended the American Academy of Art. He has traveled throughout the world in order to depict the participants of the sport, whether they are the horses, their jockeys or their owners. Pauly's oil painting of Seabiscuit depicts him going to the post in his last race, the Santa Anita Handicap of 1940. This painting was on the cover of The Illinois Racing News in July of 2004, which was a Seabiscuit Special Issue. He also did graphite studies of

George Woolf and Red Pollard. Both are wearing the Howard "Triangle H" silks. I found these to be remarkable in that the personalities of the two jockeys were captured vividly. Woolf has an attitude of confidence and Pollard has a devilish smirk on his face.

TOM CHAPMAN is the new kid on the block. Born and raised in Montana, Tom's interests were in athletics and art. In high school the art began to conflict with the interest in sports and he hung up his brushes and went on to become a Montana State Champion wrestler in his senior year of high school. His size and his athletic prowess made him a natural as a jockey. Tom began his riding career on the tough Southern California circuit and was the leading 1978 apprentice jockey in Southern California. Tom moved his tack to the Northern California circuit and took up art again at the behest of his wife Katherine. She correctly felt that his art would ease the stress of race riding for him. In 1996 Tom retired from race riding and became a full time painter. His knowledge of horses and racing has been a great asset to him in the ability to accurately depict his subjects. Tom also painted a collage of Seabiscuit, researching it down to the smallest detail. His painting also depicts the famous Seabiscuit/War Admiral match race, but War Admiral is correctly illustrated as a dark brown and the jockeys are riding with longer stirrups. The painting also shows Seabiscuit in the winner's circle after his last start, The Santa Anita Handicap of 1940. The most prominent part of the collage depicts Seabiscuit in a post parade scene at Bay Meadows, with George Wolff up.

The Seabiscuit collage is printed on canvas, using the relatively new technology known as Giclee (Pronounced "zheeclay"). This process produces museum quality prints that are difficult to distinguish from the original. Tom describes the process by saying, "Individual droplets of color are sprayed onto the surface at a rate of 4–5 million droplets per second. Once completed a 34" by 46" image is comprised of almost 20 billion droplets of ink." The Seabiscuit prints, issued in three sizes on canvas, are rightfully very popular.

A smiling "Tex" Wheeler accompanies another Seabiscuit statue. This one includes jockey "Red" Pollard.
Photo courtesy of The Seabiscuit Heritage Foundation

Although the artist is not identified, this rendition is, in the author's opinion, the most realistic drawing of Seabiscuit's head.
Photo courtesy of the author

THE SEABISCUIT HERITAGE
FOUNDATION

Ridgewood Ranch was the home of the legendary Seabiscuit and is his final resting place. It is one of the few remaining sites, depicting a time in history when a great Thoroughbred gave hope to a struggling nation, which can still be preserved. Developers have bought GlenRiddle, the farm that was the birthplace of Seabiscuit's greatest rival War Admiral. The only reminder of the great horses who once roamed the lush pastures are two golf courses which go by the names of Man O' War and War Admiral.

In the spring of 2003 the National Trust for Historic Preservation identified Ridgewood Ranch as one of America's eleven most endangered historic places. It was one of only two named which are west of the Mississippi River and the only one in California.

In announcing their decision the National Trust described the ranch by saying, "Nestled in the oak and redwood studded ranchlands and mountains of Northern California is the home of a great American legend, Seabiscuit. It was here in 1939 at Ridgewood Ranch that an improbable winning trio–owner Charles Howard, jockey Red Pollard and trainer Tom Smith–nursed the ailing racehorse back to health after a serious injury. Seabiscuit's recuperation set the stage for an electrifying blaze-of-glory career finish at Santa Anita Racetrack that captured Depression-era America's imagination." They continue, "From 1940 until being laid to rest on the ranch in 1947, Seabiscuit became a major tourist attraction with thousands of visitors passing under the gate proudly proclaiming "Ridgewood Ranch, Home of Seabiscuit."

The solution proposed by the National Trust stated, "The Golden Rule Church Association has been actively working with a Land Trust and the newly formed Seabiscuit Heritage Foundation to develop strategies for the long-term protection of Ridgewood Ranch." A conservation easement is being developed that would protect 4,600 acres (7 square miles) of the ranch. The California Department of Conservation has already committed up to $1,000,000 to purchase a farmland easement on the property, and the church has agreed to donate a substantial portion of the easement value and to provide public access.

Additionally, historic preservation planning for the historic ranch core is underway. Solutions being discussed are: "development of preservation easements to protect the ranch's significant historic sites in perpetuity, assistance with long range planning, including assessments and studies of the cultural heritage resources on the property; and community education programs, including workshops and publications with special attention to tourism and marketing. Although all of these solutions are viable, funding is in short supply."

Currently the Seabiscuit Heritage Foundation is expanding public education through historic tours, workshops and docent-led environmental walks.

One of the first projects was the restoration of Seabiscuit's stud barn, thanks to the generosity of The Willits Rotary Club. "Without the leadership of Dale Flanagin, President of the Rotary Club, and its members, the restoration wouldn't have been possible," stated Tracy Livingston, President of the Seabiscuit Heritage Foundation. The outer walls were still standing, but the four stall barn had been gutted-out and used as a print shop for many years. It has been authentically rebuilt and on May 29, 2004 there was a dedication ceremony and grand re-opening of Seabiscuit's stud barn, preceded by a docent-led walking tour of the ranch. Several members of the Howard family as well as additional dignitaries and a large crowd of Seabiscuit fans attended the dedication ceremony.

An interesting fact was uncovered while I was doing research for this book. I came across an old picture of Man O' War's stud barn. Excepting for the addition of a cupola on the roof of Seabiscuit's barn, they were nearly identical in design. I had been unaware that Howard had used the Man O' War barn as the model for Seabiscuit's home.

While the Foundation has focused on the ranch's most famous resident, the ultimate goal is to create a living museum by continuing the tradition of Ridgewood Ranch as a working ranch.

The restoration of the historic buildings continues. The century-old residence of the Howard family is currently being restored and preserved and a new roof has been placed on the huge "Upper Mare Barn" in order to delay the deterioration of the building caused by the elements. The outer walls are in desperate need of attention, but the inner walls have suffered less damage and the foundation is sound. Other sites needing immediate attention include the old Carriage House and the Breeding Barn.

Additional programs are under consideration, including a

retirement home for Thoroughbreds and a small breeding program. The latter would stress the preservation of the Seabiscuit bloodlines and the majority of the resultant foals would be sold in order to support the program and to raise funds for the restoration project. In the summer of 2005, the first descendants of the legendary stallion were returned to the ranch. Four are Quarter Horses, the first of which is First Class A.J. He is a palomino gelding owned by Cindy Rose, a volunteer on the program to restore Ridgewood Ranch and a docent for the walking tours on the property. All in Fashion, owned by Jacqueline Cooper, is the first Thoroughbred descendant of Seabiscuit to return to her ancestral home. Cooper, also a volunteer for the program, lives just ten miles from Ridgewood and purchased the mare, shipping her from Wisconsin. She also recently acquired a second mare with Seabiscuit lineage that will also be used to perpetuate the historic blood of the great champion.

The Foundation Board of Directors include President, Tracy Livingston, Colonel Michael Howard USMC (Great Grand-Son of Charles Howard), Gary Kozel, Bob Whitney and Bill Nichols, who worked on the ranch when Seabiscuit was in residence and is the author of this book. Additional members are under consideration. The honorary board members include Laura Hillenbrand, (author of Seabiscuit: An American Legend), Barbara Howard, (author of Letters to Seabiscuit), Janice Howard, (Great Grand-daughter of Charles Howard), Jeff Bridges, who portrayed Howard in the film Seabiscuit, Gary Ross, (Director of the film), Stephen Ives, (Producer/Director of the Emmy winning documentary on Seabiscuit), Chris McCarron, (Hall of Fame jockey), Knox Mellon, (former California State Preservation Officer), John Pollard, who is the nephew of Red Pollard and Richard Moe,

(President of the National Trust for Historic Preservation). What an impressive line-up!

The Seabiscuit Heritage Foundation, a 501 (c) 3 non-profit organization, is a grassroots organization started by people dedicated to telling the story of Seabiscuit through the Northern California ranch where the champion racehorse lived out his life. Funds are urgently needed to support ongoing programs and to restore ranch buildings.

One of the most ambitious and exciting projects is the duplication of the famous life-sized Seabiscuit statue. It has long been the dream of those connected to the project to find the funding to accomplish this task. Recently, benefactors have agreed to donate the considerable cost of accomplishing this dream, estimated at $65,000. Strangely enough, it took someone from England to do this. Mr. and Mrs. (Chris and Anita) Lowe are rightly described as "huge Seabiscuit fans." All Seabiscuit fans, the world over, owe this couple a tremendous vote of appreciation. Visitors will soon be able to see an exact duplicate of the "Biscuit." The statue will be placed "near" the grave of Seabiscuit on Ridgewood Ranch. A major problem in reproducing the statue was that, in order to make a casting, one of the two existing statues had to be covered with latex for a period of four or five days. The temperature could not drop below forty degrees in order for the latex to set up. The National Museum of Racing, in Saratoga Springs, New York, was very accommodating. Unfortunately, the weather was not and the statue had a covering of snow on it and Santa Anita Racetrack could not accommodate the project at the time desired. Fortunately, the Company contracted for the project got creative. They put a tent over it and placed a heater inside. The project was underway and a dedication ceremony is planned for the early summer of 2007.

The famed statue of Seabiscuit at Santa Anita Park. Sculpted by "Tex" Wheeler, a duplicate will be placed "near" Seabiscuit's final resting place on Ridgewood Ranch.

Photo courtesy of *The California Thoroughbred* magazine

This is one of the few "Carriage Houses" remaining in The United States. It is currently being restored.

Photo courtesy of The Seabiscuit Heritage Foundation

Sea Biscuit's Stud Barn, the completed project.

Photo courtesy of The Seabiscuit Heritage Foundation

"First Class A.J." This handsome Quarter Horse is the first descendant of Seabiscuit to reside on Ridgewood Ranch after a fifty-six year period.
Photo courtesy of Cindy Rose

The "Upper Mare Barn" was in critical condition. A new roof protected it from further deterioration. The outer walls are now being replaced. Note the chain around it to keep it from collapsing.
Photo courtesy of the author

SEABISCUIT: THE CONCLUSION

*I*t stands to reason that after racing eighty-nine times, certain races would stand out in Seabiscuit's lengthy and illustrious career. The two best remembered are the match race with War Admiral and his final race in the 1940 Santa Anita Handicap. However, there were others that are worth recalling. One such race was run on March 27,1938 at Agua Caliente Racetrack in Tijuana, Mexico. Earlier that month Seabiscuit had carried 126 pounds to a nose defeat by Stagehand, who was carrying twenty-six pounds less. The plan had been for Seabiscuit to next run in the lengthy fourteen furlong San Juan Capistrano Handicap at Santa Anita but when the racing secretary assigned 135 pounds to Seabiscuit it was time to look for other options.

The Agua Caliente Handicap would fit the schedule. It would allow "The Biscuit" a three-week break, it was to be run at a mile and one-eighth and Seabiscuit was assigned 130 pounds. Those were the positives. Unfortunately, there were several negatives. The race, once the world's richest, sporting a $100,000 purse, had lost its luster along with ninety per-cent of its purse money. Another negative was that Seabiscuit would have to change jockeys. Pollard was still recuperating and Woolf had received a thirty-day suspension as the result of his actions in the Santa Anita Handicap. Woolf had hit Johnny Adams over the head for crowding him in the race. Noel Rich-ardson would be selected to replace Woolf. The most difficult problem was in convincing the connections of the other horses to enter against Seabiscuit. This, despite the great weight advantages that the racing secretary had afforded the others. The second highest weight, among the seven competitors was 108 pounds. In order to convince trainers to enter, the track put up an additional amount of money to go to the second place horse. Finally the race was run. Seabiscuit led from wire to wire, winning be two lengths "eased up." The place horse carried 103 pounds and the show horse 98 pounds.

Another race to remember was the match race against South American champion Ligaroti. It wasn't just horse against horse in the match, it was father against son. Lin Howard, son of Charlie, co-owned Ligaroti with Bing Crosby and the match race was held at Del Mar. Bing was one of the founders of the track and a shareholder in it. The race was run on August 12, 1938 at the distance of one mile and one-eighth. Seabiscuit carried 130 pounds with George Woolf in the saddle while Ligaroti packed 115 pounds with Noel Richardson as the pilot. Seabiscuit won the winner take all purse of $25,000, but only by the shortest of noses. The race brought out the fans and made the newly opened Del Mar famous. The pre-race public-ity and the accusations that the race was formed simply to let Seabiscuit's earnings come closer to Sun Beau's world record caused the California Racing Board to restrict the race to a non-betting exhibition.

In the book "Racing in America, 1937–1959," Robert F.

Kelly describes the race as follows. "Seabiscuit started from the rail and immediately it became apparent that this was to be no "Hippodrome," so far as the contestants were concerned. The South American was off a shade in front, and stayed there for a mile. Down the backstretch, Seabiscuit managed to gain a slight lead, but they entered the stretch almost nose and nose. They had put the mile behind them in 1:36 1/5, very fast for that track that day. All down the stretch, with the crowd roaring, they fought each other and Ligaroti, which had the reputation of bearing in, was laying over on Seabiscuit. But George Woolf, instead of taking back, lashed at Noel Richardson on the other, and they were literally locked together as they crossed the finish line." Seabiscuit won by a nose, running a full four seconds faster than the track record.

John Hervey stated, "Both jockeys were suspended for the remainder of the meeting for foul riding. According to the testimony of the patrol judges and the presiding officials themselves, when he saw that Seabiscuit could not be beaten, Richardson reached over in the home stretch and grabbed Woolf's saddlecloth, and then his bridle-rein, thus impeding the horse and making it impossible for him to move away from Ligaroti. In retaliation Woolf had used his whip on Richardson in order to loosen his hold. The horses themselves had committed no fault."

The Pimlico Special, better known as the match race between Seabiscuit and War Admiral was the best known of all of Seabiscuit's many races. The on again, off again "Race of the Century" was one of the most anticipated sports events in American history. Howard had difficulty in interesting Riddle, War Admiral's owner, in participating in the affair. Reportedly, Riddle felt that War Admiral was so superior to Seabiscuit that it was unnecessary for him to prove it on the track, but he finally agreed to the match. The publicity the proposal had received, much of it generated by Howard, was so great that had Riddle refused to have War Admiral meet Seabiscuit, it would be considered that he feared the "western cow-pony." However, Riddle would only agree to the race if he could call all the shots. He insisted that the race be on his home turf, at a distance of his choice and, most importantly that it be from a standing start, no starting gate. War Admiral hated starting gates and was considered one of the fastest breaking horses in the country. All the advantages seemed to be in War Admiral's favor. Most owners would have resisted the demands, but Howard was so confident that he had the best horse in the world that he agreed to all of them. Alfred Vanderbilt, the owner of Pimlico racetrack, was to host the race. Pimlico was a relatively small track, with seating for 16,000. Because of this, Vanderbilt scheduled the race for a weekday when the crowd figured to be smaller than on a weekend. It was a good thing that he did as 40,000 fans showed up. Businesses closed in order to allow employees to view the race and virtually the remainder of the American population crowded around radios throughout the country. Even President Roosevelt delayed a press conference in order to listen to the race.

George Woolf rode Seabiscuit, following instructions from the hospitalized Red Pollard. Woolf had walked the track in the early morning hours to familiarize himself with the fastest portion of the track. Rains during the night had left the track less than lightning fast. When Woolf found a tractor track slightly off the rail, he imprinted the route in his mind and kept Seabiscuit in that lane, forcing War Admiral to run on a less favorable part of the track. As for the start, Tom Smith had schooled Seabiscuit in the early morning hours and he was certain that his horse could out break The Admiral. How right he was. Match races always favor the horse that gets the quickest start and Seabiscuit shocked everyone when he flew away from the start, leaving War Admiral in his wake. It was certainly a shock to War Admiral and his rider, Charley Kurtsinger and probably even surprised Seabiscuit. Woolf rode his steed precisely as Pollard had suggested, getting an early lead and then allowing War Admiral to catch him just before the far turn. When War Admiral came up to Seabiscuit's throatlatch, the two ran head and head for several strides. Then Woolf urged his horse on. Seabiscuit had the ability to accelerate quickly and he used that talent to put away an exhausted War Admiral. Ears pricked, The Biscuit moved steadily away, winning by four lengths in new track record time.

Elated, Howard shipped his champion back to the west coast. He still had two additional goals for the horse. He wanted Seabiscuit to become the world's leading money earner and to finally win the Santa Anita Handicap. He had been defeated by a nose in each of the two previous editions of the famous race and, hopefully, 1939 would be his year of vindication. It was not to be. Given a three and a half month break, he made his first 1939 start in a Valentine Day Santa Anita allowance race that was to serve as a prep race for the Big Cap. It was to be his first and final 1939 race. He injured a tendon in the race, finishing second on three legs. Heading home to Ridgewood Ranch, he was to join Red Pollard who was also recuperating from his own injured leg. It was at this point in time that Pollard quipped, "Well Pops, we have four good legs between us."

It was highly doubtful that either Seabiscuit or Pollard would be able to resume their athletic careers. Seabiscuit would be bred to seven mares that season and Pollard would marry his hospital nurse, Agnes. Their careers continued to mirror each other. Both would sire offspring to be born in the spring of 1940.

During Seabiscuit's recovery period the Howard stable was far from dormant. Howard had imported the Argentine

Thoroughbred Kayak II and he was to replace Seabiscuit by carrying the red and white, triangle "H" silks in the 1939 Santa Anita Handicap. It was just the beginning of the popularity of importing South American horses to America and Howard's son Lin selected Kayak II for his father. He was an unraced, unbroken two year old, by South American standards, but a three year old in North America. Howard purchased him at auction for $7,500, a tidy sum by Argentine standards at the time. Tom Smith used his magic on the horse and first entered him in a race in June of 1938. He did not win, but won his next four starts. His year-end total would be five wins and two seconds in seven starts. Kayak II was entered in the 1939 Santa Anita Handicap. Seabiscuit was weighted at 134 pounds, with Kayak getting in at 110. When Seabiscuit had to be withdrawn due to injuries, Smith began to seriously point Kayak II toward the race. The fans felt that Howard's chances were seriously compromised and that Kayak II could not last the mile and a quarter distance of the Big Cap. His odds went to 20 to 1.

On February 18, Kayak II was entered in the mile and a sixteenth San Carlos Handicap, a prep for the Santa Anita Handicap. He closed ground and won by a nose just 2/5ths of a second off of the American record for the distance. The public began to take notice and he went off as the favorite at odds of three to one for the Big Cap. Unfortunately, in the huge sixteen-horse field, Howard's star drew the outside sixteen hole for a post position. He broke well and settled into the middle of the field. Gradually moving up, he was in contention at the head of the stretch and made a run for it. He moved forward and took the lead shortly before the finish, winning well within himself by a half-length from Wichee. Kayak II went on the win the Hollywood Gold Cup and a total of five major stakes in 1939, finishing second in two, including the Pimlico Special. He was a wonderful replacement for Howard's beloved

Seabiscuit, but he couldn't replace him in Howard's heart or that of the fans. Kayak II, however, was widely considered to be the best racehorse ever imported from a foreign land.

Pollard and Seabiscuit had made a habit of beating the odds and they were to do it again, returning to the racing wars five days less than a year after Seabiscuit's career threatening injury. On February 9th he made his first start in a seven-furlong overnight handicap. In close quarters, carrying ten pounds more that the winner, he finished third. Eight days later, he ran in the San Carlos Handicap. Again in close quarters, he finished an undistinguished sixth. This was his poorest showing since he began wearing the Howard silks four years previously. Not to be discouraged, one week later he ran against stable mate Kayak II in the San Antonio Handicap. Seabiscuit won by 2 ½ lengths and the effort was described in the Racing Form as "Much best." Kayak II carried 128 pounds to Seabiscuit's 124-pound assignment. The race was described by John Hervey, in "American Race Horses–1940" as follows, "To many of those who witnessed the performance it was incredible. Breaking from the No. 12 stall, he was taken at once close to the leaders, from fifth at the quarter had raced into second place at the half, lapping the leader, Vino Puro, to his girths, moved on past him rounding the upper turn, and in the stretch came away with such speed and strength that he seemed just beginning to race. (Authors note: It sounds like the X Factor to me–see following paragraphs) This despite the blazing pace–quarter in :23 1/5, half in :46 4/5, three quarters in 1:11 1/5, mile in 1:36 2/5 and mile and a sixteenth in 1:42 2/5, he pulled up "looking for horses" and came cantering back to pose before the cheering throng fresh as the traditional daisy."

A week later, Seabiscuit was to make his third attempt at winning the world's richest race, the Santa Anita Handicap. He was assigned 130 pounds to Kayak's 129. His previous win over his stable mate had cost him a five-pound switch in the weights. Not to worry. Seabiscuit was famous for his ability to pack high weights and give away huge differences in weights to his competitors. His large heart allowed him to accelerate after forcing a fast pace. Five days after their race in the San Antonio, both horses worked five eighths of a mile on an off track. The track was so bad that double "dogs" were used. (see glossary) Each worked without company. Seabiscuit cruised the five furlongs in 1:00 3/5 and Kayak II in 1:01: 1/5. The pair was ready.

This, incidentally, was many decades prior to the "X Factor" discovery by Marianna Haun, aided by Dr. Fred Fregin's innovative method of measuring heart size on a living horse. Prior to this time, heart sizes were determined only on cadavers. This definitely defeated the purpose if one were trying to determine which of his racing prospects carried a large heart. Haun's two "X Factor books explains that a large heart is inherited on the X, or female, chromosome. This makes it impossible for a male horse to inherit heart size from his sire, only from his dam. A female, on the other hand, receives the heart size gene from both parents. It also explains why many great horses fail to continue a sire line, but are very successful broodmare sires. Secretariat and Seabiscuit were both examples of this trait.

Shortly prior to the 1940 Santa Anita Handicap it was announced that "Win, lose or draw," this was to be Seabiscuit's finale. A stellar field of twelve top handicap horses was entered in an attempt to unseat the champion. In addition to Kayak II, there was the consistent Heelfly, Whichcee, Specify, Royal Crusader, Wedding Call and the Binglin Farm entry of Don Mike and Ra 11. Binglin was the racing partnership of Bing Crosby and Lin Howard.

Records of all sorts were broken that day. Attendance, wagering and the number of cars overflowing the parking lot all were in record numbers, as was the estimate of the huge number of celebrities from the United States as well as foreign lands. It was reminiscent of the great match race with War Admiral. The Howard entry was a prohibitive favorite and, as was the rules permitted, Howard declared to win with the Biscuit. Kayak II had drawn the favorable number two post position and Seabiscuit was in the twelve hole, a disadvantageous spot for a horse with early speed.

The crowd gave Seabiscuit a standing ovation from the time he set foot on the track until the post parade was over. They put their money and their hands where their hearts were. Marcela remained at the barn. She was so emotionally involved that she feared she would be unable to control her emotions in the midst of the throngs of fans. When the race began, she raced for the track and climbed atop a water truck to cheer on her beloved horse.

When the field broke from the gate, the speedy Whichcee took the lead. Seabiscuit, usually reserved well off the leader, was rushed into contention and was lapped onto the leader going into the stretch. Hervey describes the stretch run. "Outbursts of cheers, shouts and screams such as Santa Anita never before had heard broke forth. It seemed as if all 74,000 throats in the over-wrought throng had joined in one spontaneous cry, on and on he came, running free and strong, Pollard steadying him and only mildly riding him, his stride rhythmic, his ears playing, his flight strait and true." Seabiscuit edged ahead, but Whichcee was game to the finish, missing second by a short length. Kayak II, running in last place for the first six furlongs, made his patented challenge coming around the far turn. He came charging down the stretch and finished second to his stable mate in a brilliant attempt to win two Santa Anita Handicaps in a row. The chart indicates the distance between Seabiscuit and Kayak II to be a half-length, but pictures indicate that it was closer to three lengths. Seabiscuit set a new track record, breaking the one set by Kayak II the previous year.

Some historians question if, had he been more aggressively ridden, Kayak II could had caught Seabiscuit. I think it probably is true that Haas, the jockey on Kayak II, stopped urging his mount when he saw that the entry was going to run one-two, but Pollard also eased Seabiscuit when it was obvious that he had the race won. Besides, the doubters fail to take into account the fact that Seabiscuit was notorious for allowing horses to come up to him and then accelerating to open up lengths on them. Remember War Admiral? Had Kayak II been aggressively ridden to the finish, Seabiscuit would have lowered the track record even more than he did.

Seabiscuit had won his final start, set a new track record in doing so and became the World's Leading Money Winner. He had accomplished all of the goals set for him by Howard and it was time to head home for Ridgewood Ranch.

The overall record, compiled by the champion, was phenomenal. He set a total of ten track records. Despite the claim that he was a complete failure at the age of two, three of those records were set at that age. He retained his quality and speed until the end, setting a new track record in his eighty-ninth and final start at the age of seven. In all, he won twenty-seven Stakes events. He was awarded a huge number of awards during his lifetime and one fifty-six years after his death. In 2003 Time Magazine polled their readers asking, "Who is your favorite racehorse of all time. Of the 8,104 votes cast, 50.3% voted for Seabiscuit and 42.4% for Secretariat with the balance divided among several.

It was at the idyllic Ridgewood that he would produce the little "biscuits," host thousands of visiting admirers, ride the trails with Charlie Howard in the saddle and die much too soon. Shortly after midnight, on May 17, 1947 his groom Sergeant Joy was awakened by sounds coming from Seabiscuit's stall. Dr. John Britton, the ranch Veterinarian was immediately called, but the champion died within ten minutes of his arrival. His great heart had ceased to support him. The farm phoned the Howard residence, in San Francisco, with the news. It was Marcela who received the call and it she who had to break the devastating news to Charles.

Seabiscuit was buried under an oak tree, the location known to only a very few of us, sworn to secrecy by Howard. Laverne Booth, Ridgewood youngster at the time, was present at the burial and reports that Howard said, "He'll show them how to run up in horse heaven."

The San Francisco Chronicle devoted most of its Sports Section to Seabiscuit's injury on Valentines Day, 1939.

Photo courtesy of The Seabiscuit Heritage Foundation

Seabiscuit	Hard Tack	Man O' War (S)	Fair Play (S/P)	Hastings	Spendthirft
					Cinderella
				Fairy Gold	Bend Or
					Dame Masham
			Mahubah	**Rock Sand (C/S)**	Sainfoin
					Roquebrune
				Merry Token	Merry Hampton
					Mizpah
		Tea Biscuit	**Rock Sand (C/S)**	Sainfoin	Springfield
					Sanda
				Roquebrune	**St. Simon**
					St. Marguerite
			Tea's Over	Hanover	**Hindoo**
					Bourbon Belle
				Tea Rose	King Alfonso
	Swing On	Whisk Broom (II)	Broomstick (I)	Ben Brush (I)	Bramble
					Roseville
				Elf	Upas
					Analogy
			Audience	Sir Dixon	Billet
					Jaconet
				Sallie McClelland	**Hindoo**
					Red-and-Blue
		Balance	Rabelais (P)	**St. Simon**	Galopin
					St. Angela
				Satrical	Satiety
					Chaff
			Balancoire II	Meddler	St. Gatien
					Busybody
				Ballantrae	Ayrshire
					Abeyance

Seabiscuit

Bay Horse – 1933

Sire: Hard Tack by Man O'War
Dam: Swing On by Whisk Broom 11
Breeder: Wheatley Stables
Owners: Wheatley Stables, Mrs. C. S.
Howard, and C. S. Howard
Trainers: V. Mara. G. Tappen, J. Fitzimmons, and T. Smith

Lifetime Race Record

At two - 1935 - 35 starts - 5 wins - 7 seconds - 5 thirds
At three - 1936 - 23 starts - 9 wins - 1 second - 5 thirds
At four - 1937 - 15 starts - 11 wins - 2 seconds - 1 third
At five - 1938 – 11 starts - 6 firsts - 4 seconds - 1 third
At six - 1939 - 1 start - 1 second
At seven - 1940 - 4 starts - 2 wins - 1 third

Lifetime: 89 Starts - 33 wins -15 seconds - 13 thirds
Total earnings $437,730
(Retired as the World's Leading Money Earner)
Winner of twenty-six Handicaps and Stakes
Including,
The Santa Anita Handicap, The Hollywood Gold Cup.
The Brooklyn Handicap and The Pimlico Special

SEABISCUIT GLOSSARY

Apprentice: Riders who are given weight considerations due to their inexperience.

Average Earnings Index (AEI): Also called Racing Index **(RI):** This index factors out inflation by comparing runners of a given season against runners of the same season. The cumulative index for all the years a stallion has been represented by a runner can be compared with the cumulative index of other sires bred to the same mares.

Bat: A feathered whip used by jockeys.

Black Type Stakes: A Stakes race with a minimum purse value of a designated amount. ($40,000 in 2004)

Bottom Lin: Refers to the mare line at the bottom of the pedigree. Also called the "tail female"

"Bucked" Knee: A condition where the knee protrudes forward of the plumb-line of the leg.

Bucked shins: A painful condition caused by inflammation on the front of the canon bone. A common, temporary injury, usually seen in two or three-year-old racehorses. Also called shin buck

Broodmare: A female horse that is used for breeding.

"Bug" Boys: A term used to describe an apprentice jockey.

Bullring: A small racetrack which is often a half mile or less in circumference.

Bush Tracks: Small race courses in rural areas.

Cannon bone: The bone between the knee and the ankle.

Checked: When a jockey has taken a strong hold on a horse, slowing him down; usually done because of the lack of racing room.

Clock in his head: A term to describe the ability of a rider to accurately judge how fast his horse is running.

Colt: A male horse, four years old or younger, which in not a gelding.

Cup races: Races which are run at long distances, often two miles or more in length.

Dam: The female parent of a horse.

Experimental Free Handicap: A national rating of horses within an age group, usually for two-year-olds.

Filly: A female horse, four years old or younger, which has not been bred.

Foal: A young horse of either sex in its first year of life.

Foaling: The act of giving birth.

Furlong: One eighth of a mile.

Gelding: A male horse of any age that has had both testicles removed.

Graded Stakes: A method of rating the quality of a select few of the top Stakes Races that can be designated as Grade 1, Grade 11 or Grade 111. In Europe and many other areas in the world they are designated as "Group," instead of "Grade."

Groom: The caretaker of a horse.

Hand: Four inches. This is the measurement of a horses' height at his withers.

Heavy track: Another term for "muddy."

Horse: A generic term for an equine animal. When reference is made to a sexual category, the word "horse" means an entire male five years old or older.

Hotwalker: A stable employee who would walk a horse in order to cool it out gradually, after a race or workout. When a machine, which can usually handle four horses, was invented, it used the same name.

Maiden: A non-winner. When reference is made to sexual category, the word "maiden" means a female horse that has never been bred.

Male Line: The line of sires at the top of the pedigree. It is also called "tail male."

Mare: A female horse five years old or older.

Match race: A race matching two horses against one another.

"Off" track: A racetrack that is not "fast."

Paddock: Where the horses are saddled prior to a race. When reference is made to a farm, it is an enclosure for a horse.

Pedigree: Lineage or parentage.

Producer: A mare with at least one offspring that has won a race.

Santa Anita Handicap: A race at Santa Anita Racetrack in California. In 1940 it was the world's richest race.

Shin Splint: Splint bones that are attached to the cannon bone by ligaments. They have no known value.

Sire: The male parent of a horse.

Stakes placed: Finishing second or third in a Stakes race.

Stakes Race: Usually closes for entries 72 hours in advance of running and has an entry fee paid by the owner.

Stallion: A male horse that is used for breeding.

Starter: (Two definitions) A horse who is starting in a race or a horseman who assists the horses and jockeys at the start of a race.

Stud: A male horse used for breeding. The word "Stud" is also a term used to refer to a breeding farm.

Suckling: A foal that is still nursing.

Track Condition–The condition of a dirt track is designated as fast, sloppy, good, slow and muddy. Turf tracks are called firm, soft, yielding, etc.

Triple Crown: The name given to the combination of the three races, The Kentucky Derby, The Preakness and The Belmont.

Weanling: A foal that has been separated from its dam.

Withers: The highest point above the shoulders and between the neck and the back.

Yearling: A Thoroughbred becomes a yearling on the first of January following the date of birth and annually changes its age on each succeeding January first. In Southern hemispheres, June first is the designated date.